Labour & Social Democracy: International Perspectives

edited by Paul Leduc Browne

Canadian Centre for Policy Alternatives
2002

Publication of this book was made possible by the generous financial support of the Canadian Labour Congress.

National Library of Canada Cataloguing in Publication

Main entry under title:
    Labour & social democracy : international perspectives / edited by Paul Leduc Browne.

Papers presented at a seminar, sponsored by the Canadian Labour
    Congress, Mar. 2-3, 2002.
ISBN 0-88627-308-0

    1. Labor unions—Canada—Political activity—Congresses. 2. New Democratic Party—Congresses. 3. Socialist parties—Congresses. 4. Labor unions—Political activity—Congresses. I. Browne, Paul Leduc II. Canadian Centre for Policy Alternatives III. Canadian Labour Congress. IV. Title: Labour and social democracy.

HD6487.5.L32 2002   322'.2'0971   C2002-903176-1

Printed and bound in Canada

Published by

Canadian Centre for Policy Alternatives
Suite 410, 75 Albert Street
Ottawa, ON K1P 5E7
Tel 613-563-1341   Fax 613-233-1458
http://www.policyalternatives.ca
ccpa@policyalternatives.ca

CAW 567
OTTAWA

Contents

Overview

In Canada and internationally, unions have been struggling against neo-liberal globalization for more than two decades. Everywhere, the things for which workers fought so hard—improved labour standards, working conditions, social protections, labour rights—have been under assault. These attacks have been repelled with varying degrees of success depending on the country. The resulting accentuation of differences between countries, whether in offsetting the pressures of inequality or the erosion of the welfare state, is evidence that national politics and national institutions do matter a great deal. Social-democratic governments have been, to varying degrees, constrained or cowed by enhanced corporate power. They have to a greater or lesser extent adopted neo-liberal policies, reluctantly in some cases, enthusiastically in others.

Frustration with compromises made by social-democratic governments, and their often limited ability to challenge and reshape globalization, has produced tensions between labour and its social-democratic partners. This has prompted a rethinking of the relationship in certain quarters, in Canada and elsewhere. On March 2nd and 3rd, 2002, the Canadian Labour Congress, with the assistance of the Canadian Centre for Policy Alternatives, sponsored and organized a two-day seminar on the relationship between the labour movement and parties of the left in Canada and other countries. The seminar brought together a distinguished international group of panellists—union leaders and academics—from Canada, Brazil, Britain, France, Germany, New Zealand, South Africa, and the United States. Their own stories and experiences, which they shared generously with conference participants, provide a rich vein of insight, instructive both by what they had in common and by what was unique. They also provide lessons that are relevant to the relationship of labour and social democracy in Canada. The seminar afforded a unique opportunity to share experiences and to engage in frank discussion about the strengths and weaknesses of the relationship as it has evolved in Canada and in other countries over the last generation, and to discuss strategies for the future.

How these international experiences relate to and illuminate the Canadian reality—labour and the NDP—was key for conference participants. These connections were made throughout the seminar but highlighted in the panel of Canadian labour and NDP leaders. These are a few of the many issues and questions addressed:

- What kind of relationship will best advance labour's political agenda?
- Should the relationship forged some forty years ago continue more or less the same, or should it change? And if so, how?
- Should institutional ties between labour and the party be strengthened, or should there be greater distance—both institutionally and in policy terms—in the relationship?
- How can the inevitable tensions between labour and the party best be managed, especially when the latter forms the government?
- Should labour change how it supports the NDP, financially and through the mobilization of its membership?
- How can organizing and education of its membership enhance labour's political effectiveness?
- Should labour be exploring new political strategies and campaigns, new forms of political engagement?
- How should labour relate to non-social democratic governments?
- How should the NDP relate to business?

The most basic question for labour is: how does it best represent its members? At the end of the day, that is its overriding purpose and only reason for being. How does it best represent them politically? Is it by being independent of any party, is it through a close relationship with one, is it by building that party so that it represents the values of the trade-union movement? The Canadian labour movement long ago said that it could not give its members proper political representation without a legislative arm. The seminar offered an unusual opportunity for calm, unemotional reflection, away from the bustle of everyday work and the emotions of a party convention. The contributors talked about how best to achieve the goals that we all believe in. As might be expected, diverse views and opinions were expressed on these issues. But all the participants agreed on the need to ensure that labour and social democratic parties and governments work together to advance their common goal—to reverse the destructive impact of neo-liberalism and get on with the task of building a society based on equality and social solidarity.

This book brings together the presentations made at the seminar. May it enrich the labour movement and the left more generally in their quest for renewal.

Bruce Campbell
Executive Director
Canadian Centre
for Policy Alternatives

Nancy Riche
Secretary-Treasurer
Canadian Labour Congress

Acknowledgements

Thanks to Nancy Riche, Ken Georgetti and the Canadian Labour Congress for their financial support of the publication of this book, as well as for sponsoring and playing the lead role in organizing the seminar upon which the book is based. The CLC's Pat Kerwin and Steve Benedict in particular performed miracles in pulling together a seamless event in a very short time. Thanks also to Pat and Steve, and to Bruce Campbell, Ed Finn, and Diane Touchette of the Canadian Centre for Policy Alternatives, for their help in the production of this book, as well as to Kerri-Anne Finn for her (as always) excellent layout work. Thanks to Helen McLellan Transcription Services and Joss Mclennan Design for their fine work. And, finally, many thanks to all the contributors for sharing their experience, words and wisdom.

The Contributors

Ed Broadbent was Leader of the New Democratic Party from 1975 to 1989.

Barb Byers is President of the Saskatchewan Federation of Labour.

Bruce Campbell is Executive Director of the Canadian Centre for Policy Alternatives.

Michel Caron is National Secretary of the Confédération française démocratique du travail.

Ken Georgetti is President of the Canadian Labour Congress.

Mike Harcourt was the Premier of British Columbia from 1991 to 1996.

Buzz Hargrove is President of the Canadian Auto Workers.

Guenther Horzetzky is the Labour Attaché at the German Embassy in Washington and the former Chief of Staff for the President of the Deutscher Gewerkschaftsbund.

Kjeld Jakobsen is International Secretary of the Central Ùnica des Trabalhadores in Brazil.

Alexa McDonough is Leader of the New Democratic Party of Canada.

John Monks is General Secretary of the Trades Union Congress in the United Kingdom.

Howard Pawley was the Premier of Manitoba from 1981 to 1988.

Nancy Riche is Secretary-Treasurer of the Canadian Labour Congress.

Steven Rosenthal is Director of Political Action at the AFL-CIO.

John Saul is Professor of Political Economy at York University in Toronto.

Wayne Samuelson is President of the Ontario Federation of Labour.

Mike Smith is General Secretary of the New Zealand Labour Party.

John Sweeney is President of the AFL-CIO.

Hilary Wainwright is a Senior Research Fellow at the International Centre for Labour Studies at the University of Manchester.

Zwelinzima Vavi is General Secretary of the Congress of South African Trade Unions.

Labour-Party Relationships

Michel Caron
National Secretary
Confédération française démocratique du travail

The Confédération française démocratique du travail (CFDT) is engaged in a permanent debate about its relationship with political parties and, more broadly, with politics. To understand the French situation requires that we delve into our history. I will evoke several aspects of the history of the labour movement, of the CFDT and of French society. There is a separation between union action and party activity in our history, going back to the late 19th century. This can partly be explained by the influence on the French labour movement of anarcho-syndicalism, a political project that rivalled the emergence of workers' parties.

Allow me to evoke two key dates: 1905 saw the creation of the SFIO, *la Section française de l'Internationale ouvrière*, the ancestor of today's Socialist and Communist Parties. The SFIO united politically all the socialist forces of the time. In 1906, the unions responded with the Amiens Congress of the Confédération générale du travail (CGT), which laid the basis for what was to become the union charter of a large part of the French trade-union movement, namely the separation between the unions' role and the party's. In a way, that was the founding act of the French trade-union movement and of the political debate that ensued in France.

The second key moment in the history of the French labour movement is the advent of the Communist Party at the end of the First World War. This brought about a split both in the SFIO and in the central trade-union body, the CGT, which gave rise to the Communist CGT and the CGT which remained within the framework of the Amiens Charter. The advent of the Communist idea in the labour movement established the subordination of the union to the party. For a long time, indeed until this day, two opposing views of labour's relationship to the party have co-existed in France: the principle of union autonomy, coming out of the anarcho-syndicalist tradition, and the principle of labour's subordination to the Commu-

3

nist Party. The logic of subordination prevailed within the CGT with respect to its activism and its concept of its orientation, even though it was not exclusively made up of members of the Communist Party, and in spite of the fact that affiliation to the union did not automatically translate into affiliation to the party.

The CFDT has sometimes been regarded as the ugly duckling of the French labour movement, by virtue of its origins and by virtue of the questions it addresses to French society. The CFDT's roots lie in Christian trade-unionism, and in particular the side that always fought for the independence of the Christian union movement and the labour movement as a whole.

This struggle for independence has been permanent. It has crystallized around various themes throughout the last century. Before the Second World War, for example, there was the struggle for independence from employers and the Catholic hierarchy. A second battle for independence was waged in respect to party politics, and this brings us closer to the theme of today's meeting. At the end of the Second World War, the issue was independence from the MRP, the political form of the Christian-democratic movement in France. At this time, the CFDT established the rule that no one could simultaneously hold positions at the same level in the union and the party. This rule of separation took on greater and greater importance, since the MRP was part of the government and cabinet, while the CFDT was more and more rooted in the working class. The principle that the union would act separately and autonomously from the party gradually prevailed, in particular in the wake of a number of major strikes, notably in the public service and the postal service.

A third milestone in the CFDT's striving for independence was the struggle against the ideology that long dominated the French labour movement, namely communism. For a long time, the CFDT was the only social, union, working-class force combating the Communist Party on the level of ideas, notably with regard to freedom of organization and action, and with respect to the very way of conducting struggles. There again, the CFDT was often substituting for a political opposition. But, in the late 1950s, the non-communist left in France was completely discredited as a result of its involvement in colonial wars, in particular the Algerian conflict.

A final building block of independence was an internal organizational choice the CFDT made at the end of the Second World War. It decided to organize workers by industry, rather than by trade, considering that all the employees of a same firm ought to belong to the same union. This led to the amalgamation of white-collar and blue-collar unions, which became general unions within broader labour federations.

Political action has always been overvalued in French society since the Revolution. This has encouraged political actors to regard themselves as the only agents of change, to think that only political action can bring about change. In this context, law has been considered *the* instrument of social protection in all circumstances. This is more than a description on my part—it is already a value judgement—but it helps you understand the basis of our thinking on these issues today.

Several other aspects of the CFDT's evolution have kept the party-union relationship topical. The first is the transition from an industrial to a social model of society. The second is the disappearance of the Communist regimes and the decline of the French Communist Party's influence on French society, resulting in the CGT's increasing autonomy from the Communist Party. Thirdly, for a long time France did not have any alternation in government. Since François Mitterand's election in 1981, we have resumed operating like other democracies do, i.e. having alternating political parties in government. This contributed strongly to making the party-union relationship more commonplace. At the same time, discourse on politics has become much less ideological. Alternation has brought about a change in the way politics is conducted. French political parties have essentially become electoral machines and have little by little abandoned their role as the social representation of their country.

Unions have also suffered from wage earners' very critical view of political parties. The CFDT itself has not been the victim of its commitment to a political party, but of its involvement in the realm of political ideas. This led to a drop in its membership and a loss of influence, forcing the CFDT to rethink the role of a trade-union organization today. The course we have pursued over the past twenty years has reinforced our will to be autonomous, but has also caused us to develop our union activities in the broader space of civil society, a space that does not coincide squarely with political society. It is a space in which trade-union organizations, the non-profit sector, and NGOs, for example, are the organizing tools of a middle ground between the state and the individual. This middle ground, however, does not only serve as a transmission belt between above and below. It is a realm of transformation, confrontation, and elaboration, a place in which social forces hammer out compromises—between unions, between unions and employers, between other forces, indeed between civil society and the state.

This form of action led to the development of our current doctrine and principles, which are based on ideas and ideology, on the choices we must make at great moments of decision—over health care, pensions, employment, and so forth—and on the actions to which we are committed, the issues over which we are prepared to fight to defend wage earners. We are advocating a trade-unionism of social transformation that neither regards politics as the exclusive basis of change, nor makes it the precondition of any change. We believe that we operate in a complex society and that we must work on that complexity, that interaction between the various social forces. To us, one of the main roles politics must play today is the definition of objectives, the organization of that confrontation, the organization of action to transform society.

A last point: in relating to the sphere of politics and political parties, we have a practical assignment coming up in France, since we are in the eve of a presidential and legislative election campaign. In February 2002, we endorsed a statement establishing our expectations from politicians and the framework of our action in the campaign. This was our opportunity to set down on paper the broad themes and orientations I have just outlined to you. I will not quote the entire statement to you. I would just like to mention two or three points. Without intruding into choices that are a matter of each citizen's individual preferences and responsibility, the CFDT wishes to participate in the public debate. Our latest view of politics is that members of the CFDT, like all citizens, are free to vote and to choose their political commitments as they will, and that it is not the trade union's business to dictate such choices to them. This is one of the lessons we have drawn from the last twenty years. The CFDT's statement to its members during the 1978 legislative election campaign was a clear call to vote for the left. Today, we do not take a position on which party to vote for, but on the important themes that need to be addressed. We ask all the candidates to take a position on how society ought to operate, on social change, on the division of responsibilities within the state, on the recognition of social partners, on the recognition of trade-unionism and what it produces—collective agreements as sources of change—in short, we ask political parties and candidates for the presidency to recognize that we are producers of rights and standards, just as Parliament is, although at a different level, and although this of course requires an articulation between these different producers of norms.

The big themes about which we question the candidates are Europe, full employment, health—not in order for them to say "we agree with you, so vote for us," nor in order to pass judgement on them, but in order to impart to them the CFDT's way of tackling these issues, its expectations of the candidates with regard to them, and, especially, in order to establish a debate between forces that have their respective legitimacy in society—the union and the politicians—so that the debate can be a source of enlightenment for wage earners in general, and the CFDT's members in particular. We are no longer trying to promote a party-political option, but seeking rather to promote a broader option for society as a whole.

(Translated from French by Paul Leduc Browne)

Kjeld Jakobsen
International Secretary
Central Ùnica des Trabalhadores

The discussion of the relationship between labour and parties of the left is very opportune. A couple of years ago, I attended the Congress of the LO in Sweden and they were promoting the same kind of debate. In Sweden, the Social Democratic Party is sustained financially by the unions and has been in power for many decades. There was concern at that congress about the sort of relationship the LO should maintain with the Social Democratic Party, because the labour movement finances the party, the party rules the country, and the government was cutting back on social expenditures. This seemed like a kind of masochism, because it looked as though the unions were paying to have their rights reduced.

I don't have the recipe to deal with this and similar issues. Beyond expecting to learn from you, my contribution could be to tell you about the political development in Brazil, which is very different than the experiences of our brothers and sisters in Canada, Europe or South Africa.

Brazil lived under military dictatorship from 1964 and 1985, but the hardest time was between 1968 and 1977, with absolute repression of any social movement, as well as any authentic trade unionism. Unions were allowed to exist, but not to strike or to negotiate on behalf of the workers. They were only allowed to praise the general in power at the moment.

However, between 1978 and 1980, we had a huge wave of strikes in the country, particularly in the most dynamic sectors of the economy like the automobile sector. Trade unionists realized that only to fight for wages and benefits wasn't enough, and that they also needed to influence politics in general. We could not limit ourselves to defending workers' rights through industrial action. There was an enormous barrier when it came to dealing with economic and social issues, like inflation and social rights. At that time only two political parties were allowed to exist—known by us as the Party of the 'Yes' and the Party of the 'Yes, Sir!'—and neither of them acted on behalf of workers. So the latter realized that they needed a party of the working class. The Workers Party—PT—was launched in 1979-80. It was not composed only of working people, but also of academics, activists from the grassroots movements (for instance there was an important group in São Paulo struggling for a better public health system), dissidents from other parties, feminist groups, students, former members of the armed resistance who came back after the amnesty in 1979, etc. Ideologically, the PT is made up of socialists of all kinds, Christians and communists, but not from the traditional communist parties, which organized themselves in other ways.

The PT participated for the first time in general elections (except for the presidency) in 1982. It was done under very restrictive rules, for instance nobody was allowed to deliver political speeches in their TV advertising. Candidates were only allowed to show a picture and to introduce themselves. So you can imagine how we performed, without experience and resources! Our pictures looked like a gallery of criminals and the introductions were even worse. Picture our candidates for mayor: "My name is Joe. I live in a shanty town. I was arrested twice. Vote for me." Or picture our candidates for the federal parliament: "My name is Athos. In '68, I hijacked a plane in defense of my country." In 1982, the number three identified the PT and our general slogan was: "Vote for 3, the rest is the bourgeoisie."

So you can imagine the result for us. Zero senators and governors. Six federal parliamentarians out of 500, 20 local state parliamentarians, one mayor out of 5,000 and around 50 city councilors. Today we have 7 senators out of 81, 50 federal deputies out of 500, 150 local state deputies, more than 500 mayors, including those of the main cities like São Paulo, and more than 1, 000 city councilors. We have concrete conditions this year to win the coming presidential elections in spite of the economic pressure and the violence we are suffering. (During the last four months five trade unionists were assassinated as well as the PT mayors of two main cities in Brazil.) To achieve this situation we had to change our language, but the sectarianism of the first years was important to build the identity of the PT, which is recognized today, even by those who don't vote for it, as a party that defends the people, especially the poor, and is not involved in corruption.

We have a chance to win the coming presidential elections, in spite of the tremendous economic pressure and violence we shall face. The mayors of two of Brazil's major cities have been assassinated during the last four months. During the same period, we also lost four trade unionists, including a member of our executive board, who was preparing to run as a candidate for the local parliament in Rio de Janeiro. We don't know whether this murder was politically motivated or a strictly criminal act. The rumours are that he was gaining support in a neighbourhood in which the local drug dealer was backing another candidate. We don't know.

But our challenge is how to go beyond the 30 percent of the votes we receive. Via alliances with the political centre? Getting the votes of the socially excluded, who are the majority of the working class today? Or both?

The CUT was founded in 1983, with the participation of trade union leaders of different political parties, although the majority belonged to different political tendencies of the PT. Today, about 70 percent of the delegates to our congresses are trade union leaders and activists affiliated to the PT. The rest are affiliated to almost ten different legalized parties—the Communist Party, the Democratic Labour Party, the Green Party, Trotskyist parties.

A main principle of our constitution is autonomy regarding governments, political parties, religions and employers. (That's why I insisted when I was introduced that *I*, and not the CUT, was affiliated to the PT. The CUT could not be, under our rules and customs.) But we are not neutral. We officially support candidates, but not political parties. By the way, it is illegal for unions in Brazil to finance candidates or parties, even though the employers are allowed to do so. But we find ways to help anyway, even if just with our militancy.

We have also faced conflicts between unions and party authorities, particularly at the municipal level where we also have large unions in some big cities. When we win such elections, municipal employees typically try to recover in one month what has been taken away over decades. The mayor, meanwhile, states that he or she was not elected to solve only the problems of the municipal employees, but to represent the interests of all the citizens of the city. We have had to intervene many times to try to create a better environment for negotiations, which almost doesn't exist in Brazil. But in case of conflict, we always stand by our members.

Sometimes, conflicts arise between the labour movement and our parliamentarians. For example, two years ago, we had to deal with two absolutely different views about the reform of social security. We went through negotiations with the government, because we thought that was our duty as a trade-union organization. But all our parliamentarians, or most of them, were against this, because they are in the opposition and don't want to give the government any chance to reach an agreement. No agreement was in fact reached, because the government did not want to concede anything. It was important, nonetheless, to show that the labour movement and the Workers' Party are two separate institutions. If we accept everything that the party wants, then we're the same as the party. Our members would begin to say, since you're a political party now, we'd better start looking for a new union to represent our interests—especially if we succeed in the coming elections.

We are two different institutions, but we can work in alliance, because we have a common ideology and a common strategy. The PT defines itself as a socialist party (though it doesn't specify what kind of socialism it embodies) and the CUT constitution includes the principle of struggle for the immediate and historical interests of the workers. Both institutions encompass a great many political tendencies. We have mechanisms to determine the proportion of each of them inside the party and the CUT. We also have a common strategy which is to defeat neo-liberalism. We manage this alliance through what we call the "National Struggle Front," bringing together political parties in the opposition, the CUT, the National Organization of Students, the Landless Movement, the Brazilian Association of NGOs, the Grassroots Movements' National Centre and others.

Without its links with the social movements, the PT would never have become what it is today. I don't have any doubt that the classical alliance between social-democratic parties and the trade-union movement led to the development of the welfare state in the industrialized countries. But this is not happening anymore. We need to ask ourselves why. What changed? What is labour today? One of the problems may be that the trade unions represent a smaller part of the working class today than they did during the 'Golden Age' of capitalism. Our membership is falling.

But that is not the only problem. The main issue in Brazil is that the percentage of workers with formal labour contracts is diminishing. The part-time, temporary, casual, and informal labour force is growing tremendously. We don't organize those workers, because our trade union structure is not designed to do it. We haven't found effective ways to organize them. But if we don't organize the socially excluded, our political power will diminish. In order to break beyond the barrier of the 30 percent of the vote we currently receive, we must win the votes of the marginalized and excluded. We need to speak their language, we need to give voice to their demands, we need to find ways to defend their interests.

Liberal economics has been defeated before. It was replaced by the welfare state. Why couldn't that happen again? Unfortunately, perhaps due to so many years of neo-liberal propaganda, some of us have been seduced by those so-called 'new ideas.' The question is: how much market economy ought social-democratic parties to defend today? How should we regard the role of the state? These are crucial questions.

To conclude, during the last World Social Forum in Porto Alegre, a good friend of mine went to visit the youth camp and was very disappointed with the speeches, because they referred too much to Marx, Lenin, etc. He thought it all sounded so dated. I answered him that it could be true, but, anyway, who is older: Adam Smith or Karl Marx?

Guenther Horzetzky
Former Chief of Staff
for the President of the Deutscher Gewerkschaftsbund

After briefly sketching the history of the German trade-union movement and its relationship to the Social Democratic Party (SPD), I shall say a few words about the changes that have come about in German society and politics. I shall then present a 'tool box' for the relationship between labour and the party. Finally, I shall talk about the 1998 election, which provides an excellent example of the cooperation that has characterized the very long relationship between the trade-union movement and the party in Germany.

Our history has always been strained, full of tensions, even hostilities. In Germany, the party is older than the trade unions. In the beginning, it felt it had a leading role in the workers' class struggle. Sometimes, it still thinks it has this leading role... There was a kind of division of labour: the party was responsible for ideology, for setting long-term goals, and the unions were just to improve the situation of workers, by fighting for higher wages or a shorter work week. This was accepted by the trade unions in the beginning. Then the party began to interfere in trade-union politics, for example in suggesting that it could use mass strikes by the unions as a way of achieving its political goals.

In 1906, at the Mannheim Convention, the party recognized the equal role of the unions and that actions of mutual interest required agreement on common procedures. We had a number of years of political in-fighting, and even several different labour parties: the Communist Party and the Independent Labour Party tried to take over the labour movement, until 1928, when the movement found its own ideology and strategy. Then we, as trade unions, began to become the political power in society. We presented a very modern, realistic economic program—much more modern than anything the party could ever have thought of. We were thinking along lines very similar to Keynes at that time. There was consequently a shift of power in favour of the unions.

During the fascist era and World War II, trade unionists, as well as the Catholic, Socialist and Communist oppositions, left the country. When they returned from exile, they were all convinced that there should be a division of power between the party and the trade-union movement, and that the latter should represent all workers, irrespective of religion, political ideology or anything else. The Trade Union Federation was re-founded in 1949 with no allegiance to political parties or religious denominations. They were all politically independent, but not neutral. We no longer had any official, privileged relationship between the unions and the Social-Democratic Party in Germany.

Major improvements in society, such as our co-determination system or the forty-hour week, have always been achieved in our society by trade unions, including through political strikes in the 1950s.

The SPD joined the government in 1966 and became the leading party in government in 1969. Willy Brandt was Chancellor for a couple of years, then was succeeded by Helmut Schmidt. They both had problematic relationships with the unions. Willy Brandt stepped down from his chancellorship after a major strike in the public sector. And I think that the end of Helmut Schmidt's political career had also something to do with the unions' opposition to his austerity program and to his policies on the armaments issue.

In 1998, the SPD came to power and we are facing elections again this year.

We have been very successful in our history when we have observed three rules:

- we had to co-ordinate our programmatic discussions in conferences and in the bodies of the two organizations;
- we had to develop common perspectives: whenever we had divergent perspectives, we failed;
- we had to act in accordance with each other, which does not mean that our actions had to be common—we could act separately, in different parts of society, and use different instruments—but we had to act in a co-ordinated manner.

These three rules are the most important lessons we can draw from our history.

Society has changed a lot since the 'Golden Age' of capitalism. In Germany, we have observed the disappearance of the 'silent pressure of the *milieu*.' It used to be the case that if you lived in a given area, such as the Ruhrgebiet, you attended the local school, worked at the local pit or factory, went to the local pub, drank the local beer, supported the local sports club in that area. All of this created a given identity. This kind of *milieu* is disappearing right now. In a way, we are the victims of our own success. People are far better trained, they go to university, they are a lot more mobile.

At the same time, heavy industry is disappearing. The traditional type of industrial worker is disappearing or diminishing in number. We have not yet found ways to reach out to young people. We're an older trade-union movement than we have been before. Younger people don't join anymore. We have a lot of deficits in organizing women and white-collar employees—that part of the workforce that is increasing in relative size. We don't reach people in small-and medium-sized companies, who make up the bulk of the workforce now in Germany. We are thus losing contact with the majority of the workforce. This is obviously very dangerous for a trade union.

Highly qualified social, cultural and technical experts in new small and medium-sized companies are the trend-setters in society. It is most important for the SPD to reach these people, who traditionally have nothing to do with trade unions. The party needs its own bridgehead into this kind of *milieu*. At the same time, it is important for the trade-union movement not to lose its privileged relationship with the SPD.

Nonetheless, elections in Germany are not won merely by looking after this new workforce, which represents just 25 percent of the electorate. The SPD can only win if it retains the support of the old workforce and gets a majority of the swing votes cast by those who are not ideologically bound to one party. The alliance between the trade unions and the SPD is thus a necessary one. This is in fact the title of a book recently published about the relationship between the SPD and the trade unions.

The SPD has developed its own mechanisms to reach out to the workforce. Forty percent of party members are organized in trade unions. That percentage is declining somewhat. The majority of the SPD's 250 or 260 members of parliament are trade unionists. Only 10 or 12 are not. The SPD has about 1,000 party groups in companies, mainly trade unionists. The party doesn't need to go through the unions to reach these groups, but can do so through its own channels of communication, even though it is well-advised to co-ordinate its efforts with the unions. The SPD also has about 2,000 'persons who have the party's confidence' within companies. These people can organize the distribution of leaflets and things of that kind. This is very important for the party. Third, within the workplace, there are structures parallel to the party. Starting on the local level, they have representatives of the workforce and elect their own board. A similar process takes place on the regional and federal levels. There is a federal convention of the association of working people (AFA). The party thus has very important parallel structures within the workplace.

The Presidents of the umbrella organization of the German trade unions, the Deutscher Gewerkschaftsbund (DGB), and of the seven trade unions meet regularly in the Trade Union Council with the party leadership. There, strategies and important current issues are discussed. Even more important sometimes are the informal contacts of the chiefs of staff of the party leadership (or the Chancellor's office, if the SPD is in power) and the parliamentary caucus, with the DGB leadership. They meet regularly and informally, and brief their respective leaderships on new dangers that could threaten the SPD-DGB relationship. In order to help the party people to have some idea of what is going on in the workplace, we usually invite party people to represent workers on the co-determination bodies. They get elected to our trade union seats within companies, while unionists are elected to various legislative assemblies, federally and in the *Länder* (provinces).

Finally, there is the whole network of individual contacts, education organizations, foundations, research centres, mass media, conferences, and contacts with important target groups. One should not underestimate this day-to-day process of working together. It is very important that people collaborate on various issues. We can only build trust among ourselves if we have common goals and common attitudes about working together.

The year 1998 represent an interesting and successful experiment. Early in the nineties we initiated a co-operative program with the Conservative government, the 'Alliance for Jobs.' The SPD was not delighted about this. But the Conservatives had been in power for sixteen years. We had to discuss policy with them. We had no choice. Every time we were to meet with the government, we (of course) privately informed the SPD leadership of the issues we were going to discuss. These meetings—nonetheless—generated a great deal of mistrust among SPD leaders. Every time we met with the Chancellor and had a joint press conference with him, the SPD made very critical comments.

Then the government made the mistake of forcing us out of that co-operative relationship. We organized the biggest rally Germany has seen in recent history. In 1996, 380,000 people rallied in Bonn to protest against the government's action. After that, we built a wonderful climate for change in Germany. The unions were really prepared to invest money and resources in changing politics. The demonstration was under the heading: "Jobs and Social Justice." Since the SPD had to reach another audience than we did, they modified the slogan to read: "Jobs, Innovation, and Social Justice." This created the impression that they were reaching out to a broader public. However, I can tell you that this innovation topic was not very important, because we really were able to mobilize for jobs and social justice, and because the government excluded us from the 'Alliance for Jobs.'

In this pre-election campaign, two things were very important. One was to organize a communication 'bottleneck.' The trade-union movement is very diverse. Its many messages could reach different ears in the party and create confusion. We told the party leadership and those who were organizing its election campaign to make sure to treat only messages coming from the DGB President's office as the official trade-union position. This 'bottleneck' was very important. Day-to-day fine-tuning of our politics also played a major role.

The election results showed that our efforts were very worthwhile. The SPD and the Greens increased their share of the vote, while the Christian Democrats (CDU) and the Liberals saw theirs decline. The turnout of working-class voters in the election was very high. We were able to show that 61 percent of blue-collar voters who were unionized voted for the SPD. Even among unionized white-collar workers, 52 percent voted for the SPD. By contrast, 42 percent of non-unionized white-collar workers did so.

Our campaign poster showed a mouth and said *Deine Stimme*, which in German means 'your voice,' but also 'your vote'—'your vote for jobs and social justice.' Thanks to that poster and that campaign 'mouth,' we succeeded in re-electing a Social-Democratic government.

Labour's Relationship With Social-Democratic Governments

John Monks
General Secretary
Trades Union Congress

I realize that in Canada you review your relationship with the party after electoral setbacks. In Britain, we tend to review it when we're in a position of electoral triumph. And when I'm asked, as I often am, whether it's a good thing that there is a relationship between the Labour Party and Britain's trade unions, I tend enigmatically to follow Chou En Lai. When asked about the French Revolution and what he thought of it, he said: "It's too early to say."

I want to talk about a tempestuous love affair that's existed for a hundred years, a relationship between two parties that on a practical level cannot do without each other, but the story is about betrayals, serial adultery, and a fair bit of dishonesty at different times. Clashes of interest abound. The battles on a practical level between the government as a big employer and its staff are perhaps one of the major areas of tension and difficulty. It's a relationship that is claustrophobically close when Labour is in opposition, and worryingly distant when Labour is in power. So, I start from the position of coming from the world's oldest national trade-union centre. It means we've made every mistake in the book—and some of those mistakes more than once in our history.

I won't go into the structures—just some key facts for now: seventy-odd unions within the TUC, just under thirty affiliated to the Labour Party. As General Secretary of the TUC, I do not have any formal standing at all in any of the Labour Party's affairs. There are four hundred Labour MPs at the moment, a huge majority. Eighty of them are former officers of unions affiliated to the TUC. About fifty percent of the Labour Party's money comes from those thirty affiliated trade unions. An interesting fact is that the Labour Party has not had a new affiliate for over twenty years. We consistently get new affiliates. But Labour has had none. And as mergers take place, and manufacturing in particular continues to decline, the number of the unions affiliated to the Labour Party is diminishing.

The Labour Party is a hundred years old, while the TUC goes back to 1868. The relationship began in controversy, with a motion at a TUC Congress. The TUC itself was called upon to form a political party, with the various socialist organizations that were around, to represent the interests of working men—and it was working *men* in those days—to advance the case for changes in labour law. But the TUC shied away from a dependency on one party, and while it blessed its birth, it left it to individual unions, some of whom were more socialist than the general mood of the TUC at the time, to affiliate to the Labour Party.

The relationship has been stormy and has nearly broken down many times. I won't go into all the crises. In 1969, at a famous meeting about labour law at Downing Street, Prime Minister Harold Wilson told the TUC team that was there: "Get your tanks off my lawn." That was no joke. It was in the immediate aftermath of the Soviet ousting of Dubcek in the Czech crisis of 1968.

So you can see that there have been some hard circumstances. There was a sense that the TUC was pushing too hard, demanding too much, and that the government was being diminished as a result. After a major row with the TUC in 1969, Harold Wilson lost office.

And then in 1978-1979 there was a huge revolt by public-sector workers against an incomes policy, in which the TUC went along with the workers, after the relationship with the Labour government, which had been called the 'Social Contract,' had collapsed. Pictures of rubbish littering the streets of London and other cities were broadcast all over the world. The result was a massive defeat for Labour in the 1979 election, and the beginning of the Thatcher years with all that meant for the trade unions, as well as for the Labour Party.

Incidentally, Labour went on to three more defeats, over the 1980s and 1990s, and during that period the unions affiliated to Labour spent £ 100 million on sustaining Labour and keeping it going through some very dark days. They actually brought Labour back from a far-left agenda of the 1980s, which had resulted from the inquest that had taken place after the election defeat of 1979.

I came to power as the General Secretary of the TUC in 1993. Labour had just lost again in 1992. Mrs. Thatcher had departed the stage and the Prime Minister was John Major, a lesser figure in many ways. I actually thought: "A hundred million quid we've spent on failure over the last eighteen years. What could we have done with that £ 100 million? We could have recruited new organisers, lots of them. We could have improved our services. We could have developed much more in tune with the evolving labour market and not simply nostalgically hoped that Labour would somehow magically have the key to turning the world back to the way it was in the 1970s."

I deliberately started raising the question—I've been a Labour Party member since I was eighteen—with my colleagues of forging relationships with other parties, including the Great Enemy, the British Conservative Party, which was not a monolith, but had a liberal wing, a pro-European wing, with which we had at least some things in common. We couldn't sulk in our tents, just because the British people didn't elect the party that we preferred them to elect.

And we started off, controversially, by inviting two or three government ministers of the liberal wing to events with the TUC—with the support, by the way, of the leader of the Labour Party at the time, John Smith, who thought it good that the TUC was shown not simply to be camped on his lawn, and dealing just with the Labour Party. It helped the electoral position of the Labour Party if the unions were not too close. He himself started a process of reform, including introducing one-member-one-vote in all future leadership elections, but then he suddenly died and was succeeded by Tony Blair, who came to power in 1994.

The Blairites had a different, more radical, agenda. They also thought that this relationship was too cloying and claustrophobic. They started to raise the issue of whether there should be a relationship at all. They looked approvingly at the United States and the relationship between the AFL-CIO and the Democratic Party. It is ironic to see how much more important union activity has become to the Democratic Party in the Sweeney era. But in those days it wasn't as close; there were many other funders and groups having a say in how the Democratic Party operated. The Blair entourage looked at that and thought that might be the future for the Labour Party too. They were aware of the German experience and that the union connection could be a barrier in terms of attracting votes among the rising ranks of the middle class, which sociologically was replacing the working class as the most numerous part of the electorate.

It was a painful moment for a lot of people in the union world. I was half expecting it, but I was not expecting the thoroughness and seriousness that was applied to it. So Tony Blair set about differentiating the Labour Party in policy terms—though without changing the basic link, they left that more or less as it was.

He took on changing the constitution of the party, things that the unions usually voted against, and he won in the councils of the party. He made clear to the country as a whole that it was not a trade-union-based party to anything like the same extent. It was different, it was new, and that was the basis upon which he then proceeded.

A lot of us think that he would have won by a landslide anyway, because people were fed up with the Conservative Party by 1997. It was time for a change. The most powerful slogan you ever get in politics is the feeling of the country that it is time for a change. He was riding the crest of that wave. But nonetheless, he has kept to the line—an even relationship between business and the unions—just about ever since. A lot of tension has arisen within the British labour movement and, I think, within the party, as a result of this.

Let me pick out a couple of issues. A key one is public services. A great deal is being invested in them in Britain, but Tony Blair is insisting that there be an extended private element in that investment, notably through the Private Financing Initiative (PFI), whereby companies get a contract not just to design and build, but to maintain and operate. In the case of a new hospital, the civil engineering firm has been able to have a contract for thirty years to run the place, manage the portering and ancillary services (and will probably subcontract those tasks to someone else), with no proper protection of the terms and conditions of employment of the workers affected. Despite some improved protections, this is a major issue between ourselves and the Labour government at the moment.

Another major issue is illustrated by Tony Blair's actions when he came to speak to the Canadian Parliament in Ottawa and told the left here to change, implying that if it was against free trade it was a bunch of neanderthals. I know that those words are thrown against the NDP in Canada. He has done the same thing in about five other countries and he has done it to the TUC periodically (although not on free trade; we are bigger free trade supporters than the CLC or AFL-CIO).

In a recent meeting with Italian Premier Berlusconi, Blair declared that there should not at a European level be any further labour-market regulation, any further pro-worker laws.

On those two issues, and there are others, there is considerable tension between ourselves and the Labour Party. As a result, some of those thirty unions affiliated to the Labour Party are reviewing the amount of money they put into it. Others, who are not carrying out a review, are nonetheless highly critical. Given that the constitutional map of Britain is changing, with devolution of government to Wales and Scotland, there is some flirting going on between some elements in the unions there and the nationalist parties, who take a rather social-democratic view of issues like public services and worker protection. But, as far as England is concerned, there is no alternative. We have not got a proportional representation system, but first-past-the-post. The choice is between the same old Tories and the rather centrist government of New Labour. As one of those who was talking in 1993 about being a little more promiscuous in our relationships (in part because I knew that Labour would be a lot more promiscuous if they returned to power), I am now advocating the link, for a number of what I now consider to be very strong reasons.

It is worth remembering what's going right—and not just focussing on what's going wrong. We've never had so many people at work as we do today. Unemployment is under five percent. Even areas of traditionally very high unemployment are doing better than they have done for years. The economy did not go into recession after September 11th and with a bit of luck it won't.

I mentioned public-sector investment. The number of public servants, by the way, despite PFIs and privatizing deals, is going up greatly. Public-sector pay is rising faster than private-sector pay. Last year, under new legislation, we got nine times as many recognition agreements as we got in 1997, the year Tony Blair came to power. Against this background, union membership has increased. No employer would be able to do a Rupert-Murdoch-type operation today under the legal framework that we have got, a big change from the 1980s.

So many things are solidly going right. And yet we concentrate on the things that are going wrong. That's of course what trade unions do. I think it was Samuel Gompers who, when asked what unions are for, replied with the word "More." When we get something, we put it in our pockets, we tick that off, and move on to what we want next. It is the way we operate. But part of my job is to say that we have many things going right, as well as advancing the causes for which we still fight.

Society is changing. It is no longer what it was in the 1950s. We can no longer take working-class culture as a dominant factor in communities. There is a more individualistic, more fluid, and—sometimes—crueller culture. And that is true for many countries, not just Britain. The average age of a British trade-union member is forty-six, but of a worker thirty-four. The only consolation I take from that is that the average age of a member of the Conservative Party is sixty-seven.

It is very important for us to address what we are doing, what services we provide, what messages we are giving. We cannot always just be bleating about all the things we have not got, because then it looks like you are permanent losers with no achievements. If the loudest noise from the trade-union movement is about all the things we have not achieved, then why should today's questioning young people, who want value for their subscription, join an organization that is failing? So celebrating what we have achieved is, I believe, very important.

We also know that we spend a lot more on our own internal democracy and conferences, than we do on organizing and recruiting. We spend more on organizing than we did, but we certainly do not spend enough. The debates go on and on internally. We are great at talking to each other and not so good at talking to this newer labour market that is developing. We know, too, that in some unions, at least, there are great debates about the correct route to social-ism. Lively and energetic perhaps, but way off where the general population is right now. It looks esoteric, and in many cases unat-tractive as well.

We know too that the top economy in terms of job creation of the 1990s was the United States. And that has given a jolt to the European Union. Although the liberal economy had been written off as a model in the 1980s when compared to the Asian Tigers and Germany, there is a sense that it is now dominant once again. All social democratic parties are looking at the lessons to be learned from the United States. Some do not go as far as Tony Blair, but then he often does not go as far, by the way, as he tends to suggest.

The Labour Party knows that it could become a centrist party with alternative sources of funding. It would not want to, because the trade-union voting figures are very much like the German ones we heard about earlier: trade unionists do vote Labour more than any other group. Workers are a very important part of the Labour constituency. The union vote is probably more important than the money or the constitutional involvement to them.

That is where we are. What do we do? I see the Prime Minister about once every six weeks. I see key ministers a lot more often than that. I take a team of the principal union leaders about once a quar-ter. We spend a lot of time now with the trade-union group of La-bour MPs, because of some of the rebuffs and arguments that are going on. All Labour MPs are members of an affiliated union of the TUC. We have eighty former trade union officers in the Parliament. That is a very lively group that we use and mobilize, not too often and not too openly, but we do use it. Labour-affiliated unions are involved in the national executive, at the conference, in the party's policy forum, though we recognize that power now resides in the leader's office, after the changes brought in by Blair, not in the con-stitutional channels of the party.

What conclusions do I draw from this that might be of interest in the current situation in Canada? Firstly, we are talking about power, not a game about ideology primarily. It is about people getting into power who can do things for working people. The minute any union movement departs from that position, the more people will look at it and say that it is a political organization first and only a trade-union operation second.

To be a trade-union operation first, it has to be talking all the time to the people who have the power, whether you like them or not: employers we do not like much, politicians of a number of parties we do not like much. Talking to all the parties, to whoever is in power at the different levels, seems to me to be important. Trying to do things in a constructive way with those people is also very important. That is not at the expense of the social-democratic party, in this case the NDP, but you have got to recognize that the NDP would need a lot of scope, a lot of freedom. Although we regret it at times, and it is controversial, we think we probably did the right thing with Labour when it was rebuilding itself, and that was just staying out of the way for a bit, giving the leader of the party scope to make changes and, secondly, although we had rows, not to bring those rows into too great a perspective.

We did not want to put the leaders in a position where they had tanks on their lawn, but in a position where they looked like they were in charge of their party. That sometimes meant keeping our mouth shut and keeping our own arm's-length support, keeping the money flowing, letting them build—we won't build that party actually, it will be the political leadership that does so with a lot of quiet union support and union resources.

I think it is also important to concentrate union activists not on political activity, but on trade-union work, on the organizing agenda, on the servicing agenda, on extending our reach and grip. Nothing impresses politicians like a growing trade-union movement. Although we have obstacles to that in labour laws and so on, that can too often be an excuse for things that we should be doing ourselves. It is important to concentrate on being positive in our own areas and making the most of them.

Jack Jones, who was the leader of the Transport and General Workers' Union in the 1970s, was asked to sum up the relationship between unions and the Labour Party. He said: "Murder yes, divorce never." I'll leave it at that.

Mike Smith
General Secretary
New Zealand Labour Party

I've called my presentation "The Hippo Shoots Back," because when I was here a couple of years ago, talking about New Zealand unions' experience under our Employment Contracts Act—I think you'd call it right-to-work law—people kept telling me about this video called "Shooting the Hippo," about a mad New Zealand example of deficit-reduction that had been influential in casting out the NDP government in Ontario, if I've got the story right. I am hoping that what I tell you today about New Zealand's political experience will in some small way redress the balance of the lessons you learned from New Zealand and give a much more positive example of what can be done.

I want to talk about two very different Social-Democratic governments. Between 1984 and 1987, I was the Trade-Union Liaison Officer working with, and in some ways against, the Labour Party in government. That was the Lange government that brought in a very neo-liberal, right-wing economic policy, commonly called 'Rogernomics' in New Zealand. Now I'm very happy to be the Secretary of the Labour Party in a Labour-led government under Helen Clark, which is left-of-centre, and very much a social-democratic government. There are two stories I would like to tell that illustrate the difference between the union-party relationships of those two governments.

In 1984, the day after we had celebrated victory in the election, I found on the photocopier in our office a document called "Economic Management," which was the Treasury blueprint for what was actually introduced by that government. It was not Labour Party policy, it was not in our Manifesto, it was a bureaucratic coup, and it was just imposed on us. I can still remember the sick feeling of horror I had when I realized, "Oh my God, what have we just done?"

In contrast, in 1999, if I can just read from what New Zealand's largest newspaper wrote on the day the new Labour/Alliance cabinet was announced: "Prime Minister Designate Helen Clark, Attorney General Margaret Wilson and Transport Minister Mike Goshey made an important social visit yesterday. Hours after the new Labour/Alliance executive was named, they went to the headquarters of the Engineering, Printing and Manufacturing Union. The meeting between union officials and a victorious Labour Party was the culmination of an operation to retrieve the Party from the heady free-market days fronted between 1984 and 1990 by Roger Douglas... The Union Movement has provided some common ground and helped broker peace between Labour and the breakaway hard-left wing of the Alliance. Many of the new cabinet of 1999 started their journey to a ministerial limousine with the trade-union movement."

So in my remarks today, I want to focus on that retrieval operation—how it was conceived, organized and implemented—from a union perspective. Adopting the perspective of Strategic Unionism, the Engineers' Union deliberately set out to get a worker-friendly government elected. We were clear about our objective. We were clear-eyed about where we started from. We knew that it might take a while and it did. We were imaginative and determined in our tactics. Success was possible and we achieved it. From a union point of view the objective is the same for us in the Labour Party as it was in 1916: to win government. Winning power is what it is all about.

To begin near the beginning: the Labour Party sits today at 48 percent in the polls. We have recently been up to 54 percent. Under our mixed-member proportional system of government, that is stratospheric polling. If we continue in this way through to the next election, we'll win government on our own, although we'll stay in coalition with the Alliance for long-term strategic reasons.

This is a government that has kept its pledges. It has raised the top income-tax rates, raised pensions, shifted state house rentals from market to income-related rental, and repealed the right-to-work law—the Employment Contracts Act is gone, replaced by the Employment Relations Act. Unions have recognition and bargaining is conducted fairly. Worker insurance was re-nationalized. There are no titles, no Sirs or Madams. We did not buy used F-16s from the US; instead we bought Canadian light-armoured vehicles for peace-keeping purposes (some people say they were over-priced, but still we bought them).

After neutralizing a counter-attack from business interests, our government is now very popular. Union membership is on the rise after many years of decline. Unemployment is well down and the economy seems reasonably well placed to weather the current international conditions. While it is not yet nirvana, the world has definitely not come to an end as some were predicting would happen under Labour Party rule.

Unions played a part in achieving this result, moving from strategic defense to strategic offense over the last fifteen years. In 1990, the National Party won a landslide victory over the Labour Party, which after six years in power and Rogernomics had become unpopular. The National Party proved equally radical in government and voters felt betrayed by it as well. However, Labour narrowly lost the 1993 election, because it had not sufficiently turned its back on Rogernomics and the left had split. The next election was in 1996. Everybody expected the New Zealand First Party to go with Labour; instead it went with the National Party and everyone felt betrayed again. The following election was in 1999. Labour and the Alliance won a minority coalition government.

We have a proportional representation system introduced in 1993. It was brought in almost by accident. The electorate had been betrayed three times in a row and the government at the time felt obliged to pass laws providing for a binding referendum. Labour lost the election, but MMP (or mixed-member proportional representation) won in a referendum supported by the unions, including the Engineers' Unions and the Council of Trade Unions. Under MMP, you have two votes: one is for the party and one is for a constituency. The party vote determines how many MPs there are in Parliament. With MMP, the NDP would have won 21 percent of the seats in the recent British Columbia election (instead of 2), to go with its 21 percent of the vote.

For us, 1984-1987 was a period of strategic defense. Roger Douglas's method was *blitzkrieg*. Plan in secret, jam policies through in haste. We had to debate the issues inside the Labour Party. We nearly won on the GST, except that the unions split, so GST is now a feature of the New Zealand economy. We defended the labour laws; that was the one defeat of Rogernomics. We did it because we united all the unions around one principle they all agreed on: no raiding. We managed to retain labour-friendly laws in that period. The other thing we did was to elect labour-friendly MPs. Every time a safe Labour seat was up for grabs, we would put in a union-friendly MP. It caused a huge backlash against unions in the party, but over time it has proved very valuable, because the party now does not see the union partnership as overwhelming, but as extremely valuable and important, and union affiliate membership is no longer an issue inside the Labour Party.

We were on the defensive again in 1987-1990. The Labour government basically disintegrated. The unions at that time were in opposition to what the government was doing and we were getting ready to defend against a direct attack on us, which came with the change of government. It was a period of industrial trench warfare. We had to defend contract conditions, which we managed to do because we put a lot of preparation into it, while we were getting ready for a defeat.

I call the next period "The Search for Unity." A political split caused the Labour Party's defeat in 1993. Had it managed to form a pact with the Alliance Party in that election, it would have wiped out National. Helen Clark replaced Mike Moore immediately after the 1993 election and that caused a huge split again. But we supported her, and for a very important reason. Not only is Helen a very considerable politician, not only did she hold the line in the Roger Douglas government, but more importantly we thought she was a politician who could win elections, and that has proven to be the case.

Unions were divided, the parties on the left were divided, and there was a new conservative party on the scene. Our union strategy was to keep our nerve and stay with Labour. We were not giving the 'Labour' name away to anybody. We developed our own policy platform based on our membership's issues. We put a lot of effort into educating members politically and it paid off. We worked to unite the left.

New Zealand First went with National between 1996 and 1999. The electorate felt betrayed again. We then went on the political offensive. We ran a campaign to defeat the anti-union legislative changes under the National government and we succeeded. We built unity across the two national union centres, developed member activism, and linked their issues to political action. We put a lot of money into policy development in the Labour Party, because left parties in opposition are often under-resourced. This was an invaluable investment. The relationships built up, the credibility and the trust achieved, let alone the policies, have paid off enormously for us. Helen still talks about the fact that we were there at a time when they did not have the resources.

Another thing we did was to develop an accord between Labour and the Trade-Union Movement. The Australians did this formally before the 1983 election. Our accord was informal, but it was on paper, and we did debate, negotiate and work through it—not just the policy, but also the implementation plan and time-line. Again, the trust that was built up on both sides was really important when it came to the election.

We have now moved from strategic defense to strategic offense. From 1999 on, the word is to go on the charge. We intend to stay close to Labour. We do not intend to be fair-weather friends. The unions will maintain those strong relationships that were built up in opposition. Our objective is to win three more terms of government. That objective is increasingly stated by party and unions. MMP has been reviewed and consolidated. It gives a natural majority to the left, so it will remain our system.

We did debate electoral reform before we supported it. A Royal Commission looked at all the issues in 1987. We believe it is good for the left, because our system of first-past-the-post was basically a rural gerrymander. If you were a Labour voter living in a small town or a rural area, your vote was basically useless. Now it is not. Every vote counts. If you lived in an urban area and it was a safe Labour seat, you did not bother to vote. Now every vote counts. The key driver for us was that proportional representation made every left vote count. The reality is that there are more workers than bosses.

There are more beneficiaries than financiers. It is Smith's Third Law of politics: 'You have got to know how to count.' (The First Law is 'Don't panic,' and the Second Law is 'You've got to have a runner.') It is simple arithmetic and it is becoming a reality in our political context, something for which we are very grateful.

We are moving to reinvent large government, to bring back central government institutions. Devolution has often been equated with privatization and removal of funding—the whole small government idea has been very much a feature of the New Zealand debate through the late 1980s and 1990s. For example, the method of funding hospitals was decentralized and based on a competitive market model. One of the election promises we have now implemented was to re-centralize the hospital-funding system and to democratize the hospital-governance system, which had been turned over to the managerial class. I think that from my perspective, rather than that of the local activist I used to be, it is about rebuilding a central government that is social-democratic and delivers centrally to those issues.

What are we doing in practical terms to make sure we have the right kind of social-democratic government? From our perspective, the union needs to stay close to the government in power. Since the Labour/Alliance government was elected in New Zealand, the relationships between the trade-union movement at the central level and at the level of the affiliated unions have, if anything, strengthened. The unions have built very good relations with the government. The effort to educate members and activists, and to involve them in ongoing political activity, is an ongoing process inside union education programs. We are talking about three more terms and are educating people about that concept, because we know it is going to take that long to redress the imbalances that were created under the neo-liberal regime. An implementation timetable is also very important. Before the election, we discussed with Labour and the Alliance the policy set we wanted to see implemented. But we also negotiated leaving some of that agenda to a second term of government. Thus, we have an ongoing, understood and agreed-upon program that will also cover the second term of government. The key components are: maintaining union member activism around the issues that are important to them; keeping close to the government so that the relationships with it are mutually respectful, negotiated, with a clear mutual understanding; but also building a common social-democratic agenda that we are all committed to and can be proud of. The message that the Engineers' Unions will be giving its members is: "We have a government you can trust, they will listen to you, they have shifted the balance of power in your favour, and it is a government you should support."

Hilary Wainwright
Senior Research Fellow
University of Manchester

Like the World Social Forum in Porto Alegre, which I recently attended, this meeting feels like part of a continuing political discussion of a really practical internationalism, which I think is a new phenomenon. There has always been international solidarity—and internationalist rhetoric—but both in Porto Alegre and here, there seems to be a practical internationalism, which is going to be crucial to showing that there is an alternative to corporate-driven globalization.

One of the negative consequences of New Labour has been a suppression of debate. We spoke this morning of pluralism. The labour movement, and especially the Labour Party, suffer at the moment from a lack of debate, although it is debate that produces the new ideas. I have visited Canada many times over the past twenty years—for socialist-feminist events, for alternative summits, to work with the NDP government in Toronto in its early days with Frances Lankin, who thought she could draw on the experiences of the Greater London Council for which I had worked—and have noted that at all of those wider social-movement events, the trade unions and the Canadian Labour Congress were always at the fore. It seems to me that we can learn a lot from you. In the role they have played in the women's movement, in the anti-free-trade coalition, and other struggles, Canadian trade unions have displayed an understanding of politics that encompasses far more than the offices of the state or the party. To use Guenther's language, you have got past the tool box in having that wider definition and understanding of politics, that recognition of the importance of mobilizing sources of political power, not in opposition to electoral politics, but in complementarity with it and in order to strengthen it.

Where do I come from politically? I have not actually been a member of the Labour Party. In one sense, I could not stand, using the language of this morning, the masochistic pain of being part of a party whose governments and leadership so regularly undermine its purpose. I am an active trade unionist, although I am not a trade-union representative. I therefore have the freedom to be independent of the party and yet work with it. I have always thought of it as being two parties. I worked in the Greater London Council, worked with people on the left of the Labour Party, but in a way I am like thousands and thousands, possibly millions, of people on the Left in Britain who genuinely feel disenfranchised, who vote Labour, who canvass for certain Labour candidates, but who do not feel that the party is really theirs. But, in a sense, I have that masochism once removed, because, as John Monks says, there is no alternative. Until there is proportional representation, there cannot be an alternative. I have never been in the Socialist Workers' Party or a party that says or pretends it can present an alternative to Labour.

I have always believed in a wider definition of politics. Here I would like to disagree with Guenther: I do not think this means that the left is not interested in power. I would love to be part of a party that wanted, not just power in the sense of getting into office, but the power to transform society. The problem of the Labour Left in Britain is that its message always reaches the broader public through the prism of internal party debates, in which it is always subordinate, so that its message always comes through in a squeaky, cracked, distorted way.

The experience of the Greater London Council, of Ken Livingstone, showed in a very small way—I do not want to overdo the GLC example—that where the New Left could actually have its own platform, not only did it have office (which, admittedly, it got in alliance with others through the Labour Party in general), but it was able to show that it had an alternative project of modernization to that of Thatcher, a project based on democratizing the state, rather than privatizing the state. It was hugely popular. The GLC was undoubtedly popular. Norman Tebbit, Mrs. Thatcher's right-hand man, said: "This is the modern socialism. We must kill it." And of course they did, by abolishing the GLC. That experience in a small way does show that the left is not just about being permanently in opposition, about enjoying the pleasure of being able to whinge and complain, but has got a practical program, practical policies for power.

Simply having proportional representation, a choice of left parties, is not the end of the matter. I have always defended the unions' Political Funds. They are a central resource for democracy in Britain. It is very interesting that when there was a threat to Political Funds, when Mrs. Thatcher thought that people were so hostile to trade unions that the funds could be gotten rid of, a huge majority in fact defended them. That had to do not only with defending the party, but also with defending the right of working-class people, collectively, to decide how to use their funds for political purposes.

The issue is not simply whether to keep or break the link with the Labour Party. Most important is widening the definition of the political to go beyond electoral politics and seeking office within the state, and to open the issue of political funding without breaking the link. The definition of the political within British trade unions has been far too narrow, to the detriment of the labour movement and working-class people. There is an amazing book that I have been reading in the early hours when I have been suffering from jet lag. *The Contentious Alliance*, by Lewis Minkin, is 800 pages of the dramatic, tempestuous love affair that John Monks described. The demise of the relationship is constantly being predicted on the right and the left. Understanding the source of its resilience is really important. Lewis Minkin argues that it lies in an accepted, deeply embedded division of labour between the industrial and the political. Even if the unions disagree with what the government is doing, or the Labour Party leadership has said or done, in the end they will accept that the party has the prerogative over the political. And even though the party may be embarrassed by particular strikes or industrial action, the party will accept that the unions have the prerogative over the industrial. That has created the flexibility and autonomy which have allowed the relationship, tempestuous as it is, to be maintained and reproduced. The times when it has been most tempestuous have been when Labour governments have intervened in the industrial, in the workplace, over issues of industrial relations, incomes policy and so on. That is when the relationship has almost broken. But of course, then, there is no alternative. You cannot build an alternative simply on the particularistic issue of rights in the workplace, important though that is.

With New Labour, however, we are in very new territory. New Labour is not interfering with collective bargaining. As John Monks pointed out, there has been employment legislation that has removed some of the constraints on collective bargaining that Mrs. Thatcher introduced. The crucial thing about New Labour is its attitude to the public sector, its positive support for privatization, its position that the private equals reform, efficiency, and modernization. There is a sort of camouflage of pragmatism, but Tony Blair's position on privatization is not in fact pragmatic. These attitudes to the public sector and privatization have signalled a change, that has happened over time, in the very nature of what it is to be political, of what the political is, of what it is to be a citizen. It is about the erosion of that social dimension of citizenship which, postwar, we have taken for granted. In response to this, the trade unions have become, though not necessarily in a dramatic way, increasingly political, not in the simple party sense, but in the sense of widening their scope and their sense of their purpose.

This government is difficult to understand sometimes. There have been some good things. Many of them are a legacy of John Smith, e.g., policies relating to the minimum wage, employment legislation, devolution in Scotland and Wales. Often some of the other things this government does undermine these good policies. Essentially, New Labour has centrally bought the neo-liberal line that there is no alternative. It does some things to ameliorate the consequences of such a course, e.g., very targeted measures to the very poor, redistribution within the working class. To give you an example: I live and work in Manchester and have been doing research in one of the most deprived areas of East Manchester. A lot of money is being put into that area of about 14,000 households. But in the neighbouring district, a swimming pool is being closed. In other East Manchester constituencies that are not quite as badly off, the same deterioration is taking place. The swimming pool, an example of a basic right, closed because the local authority is too strapped for cash. The mainstream funding, that which is really needed at a local level, is not being provided. Money is very conditional, for particular areas and particular people.

The most vivid illustration of what this government has been about—and this is not to deny the good things it has done, Labour is better than the Tories, but we should not have to put up with the least awful option, we can do better than that—is the attitude of Tony Blair and the core of the Labour leadership to London, e.g., to Ken Livingstone and to the privatization of the Underground, which seems to indicate a government that is ideologically neo-liberal to the core. I cannot fully comprehend it. On the one hand, the political leadership of the government did everything it could to prevent Ken Livingstone from becoming mayor. Tony Blair displayed more passion about stopping Ken Livingstone than anything. What this whole experience, including the more general issue of the Tube, demonstrates, is the Blair government's real contempt for the public sector, a contempt for the trade unions, and a blind hatred of the left. It treats the left as though it were all one, as though Militant were the same as Ken Livingstone, as though there were no New Left. Blair used the union block vote, an institution to which he was opposed, to try to thwart Livingstone's nomination, as well as that of Rodney Morgan in Wales. This shows that Blair will use the unions when it serves his purpose, even though ideologically he is against the unions' block vote and role in the Labour Party.

Some public services have become bureaucratic and their popularity has suffered, but the London Underground has been a hugely popular public resource. Under Livingstone at the GLC, there had been real attempts to reform it in the 1980s: a very rationally worked out cheapening of fares, investment to make Tube stations look decent, and so on. In the mayoral election in the 1990s, Livingstone and his team were proposing a well-worked-out and not extravagant form of financing based on a bond system, borrowing backed by public securities, under public control with no profit motive. He was bringing in a dynamic manager from New York, who had run public services there very efficiently. Yet the government simply said no to all this and instead wants to introduce two private companies, one of which has been responsible for the disasters of Railtrack. In the immediate, the Tube will be a public-private partnership and democratic control will be lost.

This is a just a microcosm of a broader trend. In its attitude towards public services, New Labour is foreclosing a debate which had begun in the 1970s, in which the unions could have played a much bigger role had their definition of the political been much wider. In the 1970s, they could have played a much stronger role in showing that there was an alternative. Before Thatcher, there was a real resonance to the idea of democratizing public services, of drawing on the knowledge of both front-line workers, managers and users of services to bring about change. That idea of democratizing, as distinct from bringing in the private sector, just seems to be outside of New Labour's thinking.

In response to this, public service unions particularly are electing leaders from the left—and it's important not to lump them all together. The left today in Britain, as elsewhere, is a very heterogeneous grouping. There will be some leaders associated with a more traditional 'hard left,' and others connected to a more open, connected, pluralistic left. There is greater militancy, particularly in public-sector unions, but one should not exaggerate this. Strike figures in Britain are still about the lowest they have been in a hundred years.

There is a lot of debate about the nature of the link, of the affiliation to the party, but it is quite complex. It is not so much 'break' or 'don't break.' The Fire Brigades Union, for example, has concluded that the link should be maintained, but that other options ought to be opened up, e.g., money for other candidates and political campaigns—a hybrid solution. The argument coming from within those unions for keeping the link is not so much the lobbying argument, the view that you can influence the party more from within. There is too much cultural contempt for the trade unions. The more convincing argument stems from the question: why should New Labour be allowed to have the Labour Party for itself? This argument is put forward both within the unions and within the party. It explains why a number of people who are deeply disaffected hold onto the link, while at the same time wanting to open up the Political Funds for other purposes.

There is growing support for electoral reform. In Britain this has tended to be seen, wrongly, as right-wing, because it is associated with the Liberals. But, as the New Zealand case indicates, electoral reform would lead to the party dividing. In Scotland, there is now not just the Scottish National Party, but also a Scottish Socialist Party, which is growing significantly in public support. The result of that need not be divisions on the left, but rather pressure on the Labour Party to move to the left. In Scotland, there is a very clever and charismatic Scottish Socialist MP who has been able to work with the left of the Labour Party to win legislation of a progressive kind. In the first-past-the-post system, by contrast, the pressure is always from the right. In New Zealand, it would seem that the Alliance Party was crucial to the retrieval of the Labour Party. Electoral reform must not be seen as a source of division, but as a source of potential strength on the left.

I shall conclude with a quick example of the widening of the definition of the political. Newcastle has successfully fought off privatization in the local authority. They did so by building very strong, practical connections and coalitions with the community organizations, the organizations of the disabled, elderly people, and so on, in that locality. When home care was threatened with privatization, they did not just defend in the workplace, but brought together the front-line workers with the cared-for, with the organizations that represent them. They did not only say 'No' and win support for their stance, but also developed an alternative proposal for how that service could be improved. That was preceded by an experience in which the union, Unison, had played a crucial part in backing the communities in Newcastle that had been fighting a 'regeneration' plan that involved demolition of major swathes of working-class areas on the banks of the Tyne, beautiful areas that were to be turned over to Yuppie housing. The end result of that was firstly a coalition—and I know that coalitions are nothing new to you—and secondly alternative proposals for modernization. This is where policy research is crucial. But what is also crucial is that it is policy-making of a new kind, a kind that draws on the knowledge and experience of workers, and treats them not just as wage-earners, but as producers and deliverers of a service, a real resource for developing an alternative, working with the users and people in the community. It is also an illustration of a different approach to the state, which is about democratizing the state through combining participatory democracy with representative democracy. (The Brazilian experience is the most developed along these lines.) Also, it is an approach to recruitment: the public sector union, Unison, in Tyneside has grown fantastically, because young people, people in the community who were involved in casual work, who might not otherwise have looked to a union, have seen it play a role in their own daily lives.

Faced with a situation such as ours with New Labour, i.e. a party one cannot fully ally oneself with, my conclusion is that unions must do many of the things a party would otherwise do, in terms of campaigning, new policies, education—everything short of the electoral. And then, we can rid ourselves of this masochism, which I would say has a lot to do with dependence. If one can establish political independence, then one can have an electoral relationship far more on one's own terms.

How Do Unions Best Represent Their Members Politically?

John Sweeney
President
AFL-CIO

This Conference comes at a time when we are going through a similar process internally in the United States, laying out the strategy for our own political activities in the Congressional elections at the end of this year, and leading up to the Presidential elections in 2004. In the United States, the job representing our members in the political arena is usually complicated by money. Simply put, those who oppose giving working families a fair shake have more money than we do and they use it to hammer us at every opportunity they get.

There was a time when labour and business, Republicans and Democrats, Conservatives and Liberals, mostly opposed each other, but came together on many matters of critical importance in war, as well as in peace. Richard Russell, the courtly Conservative, who was for many years Chairman of our Senate Defence Committee, was once asked: "Are you a Liberal or a Conservative?" He answered: "In a depression, I am a Liberal."

In our country, those days are gone forever. It is blood warfare day in and day out, year in and year out. One party has declared war on unions and union members and, when you only have two parties, that makes things difficult, especially when the wrong party is in the White House and, arguably, in control of the Congress. That party has also become a giant 'Robin Hood' in reverse and has dedicated itself to taking money from those who do not have enough and giving it to those who already have too much. We now have the widest wage and wealth gap of any industrialized nation. Who said that Yankee business ingenuity was dead?

In this kind of situation, two things become constant: we are forced to align ourselves with one party; and we find ourselves constantly scrambling to counteract the massive amounts of money being poured into our political system by corporate interests. The money situation and the party situation make representing working families very difficult. How do we fight back against such a system?

- First, we work very hard to be independent of even the one party that does not overtly oppose working families.
- We support moderate and progressive Republican candidates, whenever we can find them.
- We work very hard to uphold progressive values and ideals within the Democratic Party because there are many even in that party who do not share our views.

We also fight back by being more creative and aggressive in our use of our limited money:

- We get out front early with issue advertising to drive an agenda around our issues and to hold elected officials accountable.
- We concentrate heavily on grassroots organizing, registering, educating and mobilizing our members and their families by direct contact, workplace by workplace, house by house, precinct by precinct, and we do a damn good job of it, and we win.

Just look at the last Presidential election. We won. Obviously, we did not win by enough, because we lost the White House and failed to regain control of the Congress, and we are now getting beaten up daily by a very vindictive administration and a Secretary of Labour dedicated to rolling back as many worker protections as possible.

The answer to our dilemma, of course, is to win by bigger margins so that we do not have to lose in the courts or the legislatures. That is why, in terms of politics, our biggest priority is organizing— organizing new members. We are linking politics and organizing in every way that we can because we have realized that we cannot win at one without winning at the other.

How are we doing? In the last ten years, despite some huge obstacles, we grew by about 365,000 members, which sounds pretty good, but it is not, because we need to organize about a million members a year if we are to regain our percentage of the workforce. We are now under 14 percent, as opposed to 27 percent just 20 years ago.

Allow me to conclude by saying that, despite our dire straits right now, we can see our way out of our situation with a huge effort this fall. So our answer to the question 'How do unions best represent our members politically?' is really quite simple. We have to do a better and better job of organizing new members and improving on our education and mobilization efforts. It is as basic as that.

Steve Rosenthal
Director of Political Action
AFL-CIO

I would like to underscore some of the points that President Sweeney made. First, I would like to point out what our friends and our enemies said about us in and around 1995 when Newt Gingrich and the right-wing extremists took control of the Congress. The general perception of the labour movement in the United States was:

1. That we were dinosaurs.
2. That we were a relic, a thing of the past.
3. That we were irrelevant.

By and large, both of the political parties believed that the labour movement was largely irrelevant, that it did not matter what they did with unions and with working families' issues,.

Now, just six years later, we are seeing the Business and Industry Political Action Committee, one of the biggest business PACs in the United States, saying, as the *Wall Street Journal* pointed out in January 2001: "Stung by labour's impressive grassroots efforts in recent elections, business groups are planning to ask employers nationwide to help mobilize support for a business-friendly agenda." The Chamber of Commerce, the biggest business organization in the United States, is saying that they want "to match what those fellas"—meaning the AFL-CIO—are doing.

So what has happened in six years to go from dinosaurs to now having the business community say that they want to try to match what the unions are doing?

First off, if you backtrack a little bit and look at that 1994 election, it was really a turning point for us. That was the year President Sweeney and a slate of new officers were elected and brought a new way of doing business to the AFL-CIO.

Union members had not been participating in federal and state elections or, if they did vote, they voted for the right-wingers. We were trying to analyze why. What we found out was that, by and large a lot of voters felt they did not get the change that they had voted for in 1992. In particular, in the wake of NAFTA and Clinton's unkept promise of big changes, particularly in health care, working families said that the administration had not done what they wanted it to do. However, the 1994 election was largely fought around so-cial issues: gays in the military, prayer in school, and guns. As long as those kinds of wedge issues were front and centre, and economic issues were on the back burner, we felt that we could not win. A very big goal of ours, as President Sweeney said, was therefore to begin to change the shape of elections so that they were about things that mattered to working people.

Everybody talks about money and it is a huge factor. The num-bers in Figure 1 are pretty staggering. This is total union contribu-tions just to Democrats over the last few elections, and you can see how the numbers have grown. You see how much we have spent and how the numbers have increased. The numbers look so small in 2002, because the election is not over yet. Most of the contributions come in at the end and I can guarantee you that it will be close to the range for the year 2000, but $84 million in union contributions is just to candidates.

But we really cannot compete on money alone. In 1994, in that turning-point election, we were outspent by the business commu-nity eight to one and that seemed outrageous to us at the time. By

Figure 1: Total Labour Contributions to Democrats

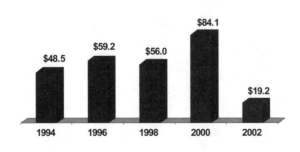

Millions of Hard Dollars

Source: FEC/FEC Info

1996, the ratio had gone up to nine to one and, by this last election in 2000, business groups were outspending unions by 15 to one. For every dollar we spent, they spent $15. With the changes in the campaign finance law on the horizon now, and everybody reaching out to try to raise as much money as they can, we expect that, in this next election, business groups will outspend labour by at least 20 to one. For every dollar that we spend, they will spend $20.

As the saying goes, "they have the money, but we've got the people." Yet, for years and years and years, we got away from the notion of mobilizing people, got more into the money competition and thought that we could just write cheques. I do not know about the situation here, but I can tell you about the number of union meetings that I went to over the years, where the local union president would stand with his/her arm around the local candidate and hand the latter a cheque. Somebody would take a photograph, which would run in the local union newsletter, and that was about the extent of our political action in too many places.

We will never be able to compete with the business community in contributions. We have to try to begin to compete by mobilizing people.

Figure 2 shows what happened over the last three elections.

- In 1994, union members voted 60 percent for the Democrats and 40 percent for the Republicans.

Figure 2: Union Vote for House Democrats

	D	R	Margin
2000	69	29	+40
1998	67	30	+37
1996	68	32	+36
1994	60	40	+20

Source: VNS, Hart Research

- By 1996, by beginning to change the way that we did our business, we moved those numbers to 68 percent for the Democrats and 32 percent for the Republicans.
- By 1997, it was 67-30 and, in this last election, it was all the way up to 69-29, or a 40-point difference. We doubled the margin of how union members vote, over just a six-year-election period, three election cycles.

We start off with a leg up. Union members like their unions, by and large. They feel very strongly about them. That is the number one factor in all of the research that we have done. A second point is that about 84 percent of our members said that they expect the union to be involved in legislation and political activity, and that they want to hear from the union on those issues. The third key ingredient is that 79 percent of union members tell us that they are more likely to support a candidate backed by the union. That does not mean that they will automatically vote for whomever the union has endorsed. However, as they decide whether or not to vote, they want to know who the union supports.

We also knew, from some of the research that we had done, that 76 percent of union members who got information from the union at their workplace, for example in the form of flyers, voted for the union-endorsed candidate in one of our elections. As we began to do more one-on-one contact, we found that union members were responding very, very warmly to it. The bad news was that, at that stage of the game, only 11 percent of our members said that they were actually being contacted by the union at work. There was therefore a great opportunity for us to go and increase those numbers.

In 1992, union members represented about 17 percent of the voting-age public in the United States, but accounted for 19 percent of the vote. By 1996, we had increased the union's share of the vote to 23 percent. In this last election, it was 26 percent. Non-union voters have largely stayed home—15.5 million fewer non-union voters participated in the last three elections. Bucking that national trend, we have mobilized 4.8 million more voters from union households.

Figure 3: The Union Difference for Al Gore

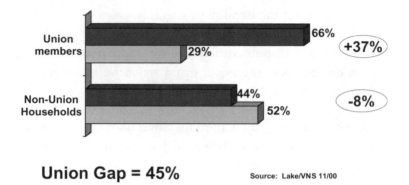

Union Gap = 45%

Source: Lake/VNS 11/00

Figure 4: The Union Difference for Gore–White Men

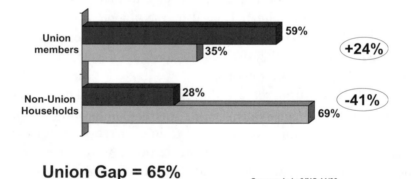

Union Gap = 65%

Source: Lake/VNS 11/00

Figure 5: The Union Difference for Gore–White Women

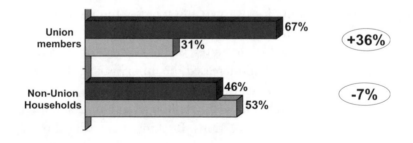

Union Gap = 43%

Source: Lake/VNS 11/00

Our program consisted of helping union members to understand what was at stake in the elections and then to participate.

Having encouraged them to participate, our next challenge was to try to make sure union members supported the union-endorsed candidate. A look at some of the numbers from the last Presidential election, shows that Al Gore lost the non-union vote, nationwide, by 8 percent. He won union voters by 37 percent. In other words, union voters voted 66 percent for Gore and 29 percent for Bush (see Figure 3). That is a 45-point difference between non-union voters and union voters.

The Democratic Party has a big problem winning white male voters, yet white men in unions voted for Gore, 59-35. White men who were not in unions voted for Bush, 69-28. A huge difference (see Figure 4). Among white women, it is the same deal, 67-31 for Al Gore. Gore lost non-union women by 7 percent. There is a lot of talk in the United States about a gender gap and how women are voting for Democrats. That is not really true. It is *union women* who are making the difference. It is a *union gap*, not a gender gap (see Figure 5).

Among people of colour, as strong as the numbers were for Gore overall, 76 percent of African Americans, Asian-Pacific Americans and Latinos voted for Gore in non-union households. In union households, it was all the way up to 83 percent (see Figure 6). Older voters over 65 in unions voted 73 percent for Gore, 73-22; he lost older non-union voters by 3 percent (see Figure 7).

You can look across the board and see this in virtually every demographic group. If you took away from Gore all the states in which he only won on the strength of union votes, the election would not have been close at all. Bush would have won the election by 363 electoral-college votes to 175.

In Michigan, in the 2000 election, the winner won with 72 percent of the union vote. She lost all of the non-union voters by 20 percent, but was still able to win the election thanks to a big enough union turnout. The United States Senate is now controlled by the Democrats, 51-49, but, without the union vote, the Republicans would control the Senate today 61-39.

Figure 6: The Union Difference for Gore–Minorities

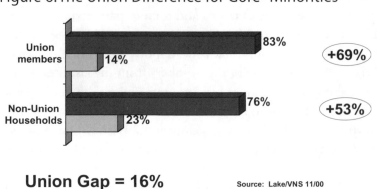

Union Gap = 16%   Source: Lake/VNS 11/00

Figure 7: The Union Difference for Gore–65 and Older

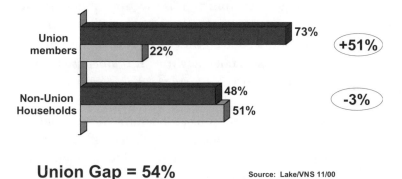

Union Gap = 54%   Source: Lake/VNS 11/00

Figure 8: Impact of Member Contact–Vote for Al Gore

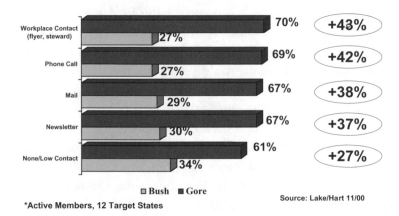

*Active Members, 12 Target States   Source: Lake/Hart 11/00

We found that union members were increasingly likely to respond to the union appeal the more personal their form of contact with the union became. The bottom two bars of Figure 8 shows union members who told us that they hardly heard from the union at all during the election. They voted 61-34 for Gore. They got some information, but generally did not feel like they were receiving a lot from the union. Going up the chart, one sees union members who said that they had received political information from union newsletters. Among these voters, Gore won by a 37-point margin. Getting mail from the union, raised the latter to 38 points, while getting a phone call from the union, lifted it to 42 points. Where union members were contacted one on one, got workplace flyers, and had a lot of interaction with the union, the margin went up to 70-27 (see Figure 8).

As common sense would suggest, the frequency of members' contacts with their union also had a considerable impact. Among those who told us that they had heard from the union once or not at all, the margin was 27 points. By contrast, those who were contacted four or more times by the union, voted for the union-endorsed candidate by a 42-point margin.

Why is the union program working?

- We are engaging members in the process while other people are dropping out; and
- We have separated the union program from the party program.

In other words, we have said to the candidates: we are going to mobilize union members. Our job is to try to bring more working people into the process. If we do that right and if we educate union members around the issues, they will support the right candidates, but we are not the party; we are the labour movement.

I came here yesterday from a meeting with one of our candidates for Governor. He was saying he needed more union volunteers in his campaign. But I replied that he would not see union volunteers in *his* campaign, but rather in the *union* campaign, running the *union* program. If we do this right, it will mean that somewhere in the neighbourhood of 40 percent of the votes in that state will come from union voters. Unfortunately, it is a struggle to get candidates to understand this.

We no longer tell our members who to vote for. Instead, we are telling them where the candidates stand on the issues and letting them decide for themselves. We are giving them the information that they need to cast an educated vote, and then using all of the tools that we have to communicate with union members.

Getting out the vote is a big issue in the United States, because only about half of all Americans are registered to vote, and then only about another half participate in elections. About a quarter of the eligible voters actually decide elections in the United States, so we are constantly struggling to get union members to vote.

The first things the recently elected Democratic Governor of New Jersey did were to sign:

- a labour agreement to say that all of the construction projects in the state would be done with union labour; and
- an Executive Order saying that all of the uniforms purchased by the state would have to have a union label in them.

Despite the fact that he is facing a $2.8 billion deficit, he is working with the state employees' unions there and is supporting unions that are trying to organize. He is very strong on our issues. I point this out, not just because he is good, but because we went into that

Figure 9: These are real numbers folks...

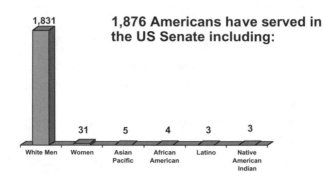

1,876 Americans have served in the US Senate including:

1,831 — White Men
31 — Women
5 — Asian Pacific
4 — African American
3 — Latino
3 — Native American Indian

election with some very clear goals. We reckoned that if we could turn out 73 percent of union members, and get two-thirds of them to vote for him, we would deliver 536,000 votes to him—and he knows it. As he begins to plan for his re-election, three years down the road, he wants to ensure that that base is bigger. Politicians are beginning to understand that they need to help us to figure out ways to build the labour movement.

We have set up a ten-point program. It is basically to get every local union, in these targeted states and communities, to get on board with the same program of contacting union members. We have had a marked increase in this respect over the last couple of elections. As I said before, we went from 11 percent of union members, who were contacted at work in the 1998 election, to 45 percent in the 2000 election. In every category, we have managed to increase union participation in this type of program.

The last thing that I want to point out is that Members of Congress in the United States are not exactly like the people in this room:

- 181 Members of Congress are business people or bankers;
- 172 of our Members of Congress are lawyers;
- 65 percent of our Members of Congress have advanced degrees;
- fewer than 1 percent of Americans are millionaires, but almost 30 percent of the Members of Congress are.

Figure 10: ... we're not kidding

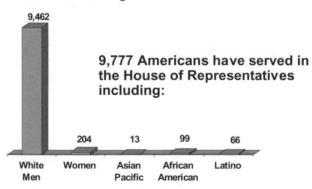

-The 2000 election added 41 new members: 32 white men, 7 women, 1 African American and 1 Asian Pacific American
-This was a net gain of 3 women and 1 Asian Pacific American

Since the foundation of the United States, 1,876 Americans have been elected to the United States Senate. Of them, 1,831 have been white men, 31 women, 5 Asian-Pacific Americans, (thanks to Hawaii), 4 African Americans, 3 Latinos, 3 Native American Indians. The House of Representatives of the United States does not look any more like the rest of our country (see Figures 9 and 10).

Part of what we are trying to do now is to change that and figure out how we begin to elect more women and people of colour—more workers—to public office in order to begin to get people elected at every level of government so that we have a seed bed of folks to move up the chain as we go along. We established a program initially called '2000 in 2000,' aimed at electing union members to office. Over the last few years, we have elected 2,500 union members. We are winning about 70 percent of our races.

We need to change the environment so that workers can organize again, and that is the anchor of our political program. And we need politicians, and particularly Democrats, to take a much more aggressive role in supporting union organizing; otherwise, they are doomed and so are we.

Zwelinzima Vavi
General Secretary
Congress of South African Trade Unions

Our own experience and international developments have shown that no trade union can avoid political struggles if it is to bring tangible benefits to its members. Yet, a political engagement holds many complex challenges and opportunities for the trade-union movement. Perhaps one of those challenges is how to balance shop floor struggles and broader political struggles.

If not carefully managed, this can produce an imbalance—over-reliance on political deal-making, and abandonment of the trade union base and shop floor struggles. A union movement that relies exclusively on political deals and lobbying under-estimates its power and is generally reluctant to use power to tilt the balance of forces in favour of the interests of its members. As such, it becomes part of the elite that has a stake in maintaining the status quo.

The South African trade-union movement, the Congress of South African Trade Unions (COSATU) in particular, has through years of struggle, learned to combine workplace struggles with broader political struggles. From its inception, COSATU recognized and understood that workplace apartheid was linked to the broader political system of apartheid colonialism. At the same time, COSATU recognized that it would not on its own defeat national oppression and had to enter into alliances with a range of other forces, in particular the liberation movement, to do so. It is in this vein that COSATU became a key component of the struggle for liberation. At the same time, it did not abandon workplace struggles—in fact workplace grievances were utilized to mobilize the workers in the broader political struggle and to change the material reality of many South African workplaces. So, workers' workplace struggles were knitted together with other sectoral grievances and became a national contradiction that the National Democratic Revolution had to address as one of its key objectives. This historical position has put COSATU in a position of strength politically.

Eight years after the first democratic elections in South Africa, COSATU has not retreated to a narrow trade-union movement concerned solely with workplaces issues. Going into the transition, the trade-union movement was faced with two stark choices: *retreat from the political terrain and revert to a narrow trade union role or continue to play an active political role whilst ensuring that the transition begins to deal with some of the contradictions referred to above.* COSATU opted for the latter option for the simple reason that even in a democratic society, workplace struggles and political struggles cannot be divorced from one another.

In time, experience has vindicated the option chosen by COSATU. Its strategy of engagement in the political terrain to shape policies and legislation has paid off for the working class. The trade-union movement has played an active role in shaping economic policy. As is well known, the latter has been a key political debate in South Africa with the government turn to the right in macroeconomic policy. COSATU's achievements and setbacks on the policy terrain are recorded in a booklet entitled *Accelerating Transformation—The First Term of Governance*, which can be downloaded from the COSATU website: www.cosatu.org.za

Trade unions, by nature, are not political parties, but form alliances with political formations. In keeping with its own recognition that trade unions or workers on their own cannot deliver liberation or a better life for all, COSATU formed what is known as the tripartite alliance with the African National Congress (ANC) and the South African Communist Party (SACP). This strategic alliance liberated South Africa and spearheads the country's transformation process.

There are prerequisites to any alliance between a trade union and political parties, in particular once those political parties win political power. The trade-union movement has to be strong both organizationally and politically—after all, without power you cannot negotiate or force a deal. The trade-union movement must jealously guard its independence and develop a willingness to stand firm on matters of principles or issues that will have a negative impact to members. The trade-union movement must develop an array of tactical alliances with a range of civil society organizations, so that it learns to have a broad approach to issues and at the same time makes it difficult to be isolated. There have to be rules and structures that govern its involvement in the determination of policy, otherwise it ends up being used as a vote catcher by the political party. The trade union must have a capacity to engage in complex transformation issues at the policy level. COSATU has mastered most of these prerequisites and failed on a few of them, notably the issue of developing rules and structures with the governing party so that it can have a direct influence on policy formulation.

There is no substitute for struggle and engagement. In a nutshell, COSATU has combined a multi-pronged strategy of forming strategic and tactical alliances. It has also developed its capacity to formulate policies and maintained its ability to mobilize members in support of its demands. Equally important, COSATU unions still embark on struggles to represent workers on the shop floor for better working conditions. Without that, no trade union can survive. The central argument being articulated here is that trade unions can represent members' political interests by observing the following rules:

- It must articulate clear policy positions around which it can galvanise its members;
- Secondly, in forming political alliances it must choose political parties that can best represent workers' interests, but who are also capable of winning an election;
- Thirdly, it must never relinquish its ability to mobilize its members and society in broad struggles to achieve its aims—the boardroom must be combined with mass struggle;
- Fourth, members should be actively involved in shaping the positions of the trade-union movement and internal democracy must be guarded jealously;
- Lastly, trade unions must continue to represent workers' interests at the shop floor.

John Saul
Professor
York University

How does labour best represent its members politically? When you look at the South African case, it becomes apparent—and we have heard that already in Comrade Vavi's presentation—that the way in which COSATU has primarily sought to represent its members politically is through the alliance that it has forged with the ANC, although a broader range of tactics and strategies have also been deployed. Perhaps Mr. Vavi has been slightly diplomatic in some of the things that he has said; his own difficulties in South Africa to some degree belie the picture that he is giving, although he made it very clear that the marriage that has emerged in South Africa between the Liberation Movement, the ANC, and the trade unions is not entirely happy.

As somebody said to me: it is all very well that the marriage should continue and that there is no divorce, but what happens if the relationship involves spousal abuse? If you want to press the metaphor that far, there are some signs that the ANC's drift to the right is not so much a *drift* as a *forced march* to the right, towards a neo-liberal socio-economic strategy that has involved the abuse of its partner, the labour movement.

A look at Africa today—Africa generally, not just South Africa—makes it immediately apparent that Africa has no scope for development within the frame of the global capitalist system, as it currently exists. Thanks to structural adjustment and various kinds of bullying by the World Bank, the IMF, and various Western governments, Africa's weak economies are being forced to play on an unequal, unlevel playing field, which they cannot do. They are being ripped off in the process by global capitalism.

It is impossible to avoid the question in Africa as to whether a capitalist strategy of development actually works. One can say till the cows come home that the choice between capitalism and socialism is old hat, that it has been displaced by history, and so on and so forth, but, if you are in Africa, you cannot avoid facing that question. My colleague Greg Albo at York University has said that the choice globally—but certainly the choice in Africa—may well be between a Utopian capitalism and a realistic socialism.

The need to transform global, economic structures and African societies in a leftward direction is paramount, and many more Africans are beginning to realize that there is no way forward within the structures of global capitalism that currently exist. The history of Africa has placed it at the receiving end of a system that does not give it much scope for development by following standard economic models. In Africa at least, the question of socialism versus capitalism actually has to be on the agenda and we cannot shuffle it aside by saying that the Soviet Union did not work—if that was your idea of socialism—or that the Berlin Wall has fallen.

In South Africa, these questions are posed in a particularly dramatic way. As most of you will know, South Africa is without doubt the most developed economy in Africa. But even South Africa's position within the global economy is not a positive one. It cannot easily be cured by the neo-liberal strategies that are being urged upon all governments in Africa. Truth to tell, the ANC has chosen a pretty unqualified, neo-liberal, economic strategy.

I began a recent article about South Africa in *Monthly Review* in the following way:

> A tragedy is being enacted in South Africa, as much a metaphor for our times as Rwanda and Yugoslavia, and even if not so immediately searing of the spirit, it is perhaps a more revealing one for, in the teeth of high expectations arising from the successful struggle against a malignant apartheid state, a very large percentage of the population, among them many of the most desperately poor in the world, are being sacrificed on the altar of the neo-liberal logic of global capitalism. There is absolutely no reason to assume that the vast majority of people in South Africa will find their lives improved by the policies that are being adopted, in their name, by the President of the African National Congress govern-

ment. Indeed, something quite the reverse is the far more likely outcome.

If that is true, or partly so, why is it happening? Given the influence of the global economy, it could be argued that South Africans really have no choice but to follow that route. Perhaps those in power in South Africa, like some Congressmen in the United States, find it more comfortable and in their own interests to follow the line of least resistance. While the economic gap between black and white has narrowed somewhat in South Africa, the gap between rich and poor is widening. That means that some blacks are moving into the upper circles of wealth, but that most blacks find their incomes falling. The unemployment rate is rising rapidly. A minimum number for unemployment in South Africa is 25 percent. Some studies put it at 45 percent or 50 percent.

This is an economy in difficulty. It is not clear that neo-liberalism offers a viable way forward, with its prescription to open the economy up even further, to privatize a wide range of public assets and services, and to legislate increased labour flexibility (i.e. vulnerability to capitalism)—moves partly blocked by COSATU.

Where does COSATU fit in this picture? Its marriage with the ANC was not immediate. For many years, it kept its own counsel politically. Even when the UDF, which was much closer to the ANC, emerged in the 1980s, COSATU did not join it. It was not until the transition period that COSATU forged its alliance with the ANC.

The marriage has been stormy. COSATU has provided the electoral punch, in terms of organization, bodies and personnel, that has enabled the ANC to win its elections. There is no doubt about that. COSATU's actions have led to the modification of what would otherwise be very stern labour legislation. But in terms of economic policy, COSATU has not, by and large, been able to stop the march of the ANC towards a neo-liberal strategy, although it has been critical of it.

The 'GEAR' strategy, which replaced the RDP as the ANC's main strategy, is essentially a very extreme, neo-liberal strategy for managing the entire economy. In introducing it, Thabo Mbeki, then

Vice-President and now President of the ANC, said, somewhat ironically, but meaningfully: "Just call me a Thatcherite."

Comrade Vavi wrote at the time: "The economy is not working for us. GEAR is not working. How can we support this? This is a jobless bloodbath." Those are the words he used. This is what is happening in South Africa.

In the year 2000, when I was working in South Africa, four million workers there stayed home from work to protest against the government's policies. The streets of Johannesburg, Durban and Cape Town were jammed with workers demonstrating. Other unions have stood up as well. The Metal Workers occasionally raised questions about the need for a socialist strategy. The Teachers' Union has been very critical of educational policy in South Africa. The Municipal Workers have been a major force in trying to resist the sweeping privatization that is taking place in South African communities.

What is their reward for that? They have been chastised at COSATU meetings, in very strenuous terms, by Mandela, Mbeki and others, as ultra-leftists, as wreckers, as people who are trying to destroy the economy in the name of some abstract, socialist cause, et cetera, et cetera. This is an abusive relationship in many ways.

It is obviously not for me to say whether the benefits of staying in that relationship outweigh the costs. Mr. Vavi has already said that it is not a seamless relationship, and any reading of the situation in South Africa reinforces that view. In South Africa, this has raised the question of alternative ways of representing union members politically. We have heard today about the other alliances COSATU is forging with groups in civil society. This is crucially important for understanding what is happening not only in South Africa, but in Canada too.

When I was working in South Africa, I spoke with many unionists and others about what was happening. To put it mildly, there was scepticism about the overall economic strategy being pursued by the ANC, as well as about the nature of the alliance forged between the latter and the unions. Of course, it is not so easy to walk away from the ANC. Despite its most recent policies, the latter has earned considerable legitimacy as the major architect of the anti-apartheid struggle and the change that has taken place in South Africa. Its political legitimacy and control make it hegemonic. It is thus not easily challenged.

Furthermore, although some people believe it would be better to walk away from the ANC, believing there is nothing in it for them, many people in COSATU and elsewhere do not want to do so. They believe it is their ANC too. Just because the group now in charge has taken this economic line, it does not follow that others do not have a stake in the ANC as well, and a right to expect a different kind of policy from it. They seek ways of bringing pressure to bear on the ANC, without assuming that the latter is always going to be advancing their interests—Comrade Vavi made this clear. The talk, in certain circles at least, is therefore very much about the need for a small 'A' alliance, with the trade unions and other groups in civil society—women's groups, environmental groups, community action groups and the like.

This kind of politics has become ever more important in the discussions that are taking place in South Africa. It is not really enough to get 'power,' although it is nice to have and probably essential. The question is rather, as we are gaining power, to what degree we have to build up the institutions to pressure those who hold power in our name to do what we would like to see them do? How do we establish a movement that keeps their feet to the fire? Without this, one gets shuffled into the category of special interests and faces the rhetoric of 'the government of all of the people.'

Power can be rather seductive unless we unpack it and look at the way it actually works in practice. That is one of the key lessons of the debate currently taking place about the complementary alliances to the big 'A' alliance between COSATU and the ANC. It is not for me to say whether this will bring pressure to bear in, through, and on the ANC, or whether it will eventually lead to another kind of political formation to the left of the ANC.

But it is a question that is posed when you are faced with a government that has moved starkly to the right and to whom you come more or less cap in hand, after having been a major force in putting them into power. This question cannot be shirked, anymore than the question of the kind of economic strategy that would actually work in South Africa.

Slowly, but surely—trade unionists are saying this all of the time—we have to reactivate the language of socialism to figure out how to deal with this global economy that is imposing results and policies on us that are not in our interest. This is a question of realistic socialism versus utopian capitalism. A capitalist revolution in Africa is a utopian concept. Socialist development is not easy. It is hard to escape the grip of a neo-liberal economic and political strategy. What it means remains to be worked out in practice. But the challenge here is increasingly evident.

It is possible to be quite cynical about this. The Polish-American political scientist, Adam Przeworski, came up with this phrase that haunts me on nights when I cannot sleep: "Capitalism is irrational, socialism is unfeasible and, in the real world, people starve. The conclusions that we have reached are not encouraging ones." To put it mildly, if that were where you were at, you would be very depressed indeed.

In Africa, if you think capitalism will positively transform Africa—as the Canadian government is going to claim at the G-8 summit—then I think that you are wrong. Most of the people I have talked to in COSATU also think that you are wrong. What that means in practice is another question. However, it cannot simply that 'we have to be where the electorate is.' That is partially true. But it is also a very static view of where people can be at politically. It suggests that we cannot begin, through various political means, to raise the level of popular understanding and commitment to various, much more dramatic, alternatives.

When I was in South Africa, I spoke at great length with various people involved in these questions and I began to introduce Sam Gindin's idea of creating a structured movement, not a party, but more than an alliance, one that begins to pull together a range of forces in society, but does not for the moment raise the party question. In the long run, would a movement that began to tie together many Canadians struggling in their own ways, and principally the trade unions, eventually lead to the creation of a new political formation? Would it be a way of putting pressure on the NDP and the Liberal Party?

In South Africa, that question is open too. There are not very many people saying that the alliance should be smashed and a new left party built. It would not be easy to do. As Comrade Vavi has pointed out, there are many more people saying that it is time to figure out a way to hold the ANC's feet to the fire and that trade unions alone cannot do it, because they are going to be dismissed as just another special interest. Instead, it is necessary to build a movement of churches and all of the groups I have been mentioning, and to begin to become effective players.

There is a need for realism, but there is also a need for a revitalization of left politics, and that is as true in Canada, as it is in South Africa, the United States and everywhere else.

Applying the Lessons
to the Canadian Experience

Mike Harcourt
Premier of British Columbia (1991 to 1996)

I am from British Columbia where the body snatchers have taken over the Liberal Party. It is a pretty grim scenario. I was pleased to hear from Mike Smith about how the New Zealand Labour Party recovered from the body snatch that happened when Roger Douglas and crew shanghaied it. We are dealing with something very, very similar in British Columbia, with some tragic consequences for some very vulnerable people, not just trade union contracts being ripped up, but:

- Blind people seeing public funds for books in braille and tapes being cancelled;
- Seniors' bus passes being eliminated;
- Single women on welfare having to go out and work when there is no child care for their children; and
- The $200 a month that the disabled used to be able to earn above and beyond their disability allowance being cut.

These are examples of the damage that is being inflicted on the very vulnerable in our society, on top of teachers and nurses ordered back to work and contracts being ripped up in the public sector. We are feeling the impact of not having a New Democrat government.

In this context, how do we build support? We are down and out in large parts of the country. In British Columbia, we are now down to two seats. We are at 8 percent nationally, with 13 seats. Yet, we have a history of being resilient. We have seen Saskatchewan go down to two seats and then come back. The same thing happened a couple of times in Manitoba. As Tommy Douglas used to say: "Bleed awhile and pick ourselves up and move on."

What can we learn from our history? The issue is not just the relationship between the party and labour, and between labour and government, or between social-democratic governments. It is also:

- Why we do not resonate with the people?
- How do we relate to them?

- How do we get away from the pendulum politics that we are going through in British Columbia, where we swing away out to the right and swing over into some adventuristic left areas, as we did in the last little while; and
- How do we get to the issues that are really important to people?

We do not really need to raise the consciousness of people; rather, we have to go where they are. I started off as a store-front lawyer, stopping freeways, and I learned from Saul Alinsky, the great organizer in Chicago, who said that there are two things that you have to remember:

- You cannot organize apathy. If people are apathetic, you are dead. They have to be angry, fearful; and
- You have to go to where they are, address what is important to them, and then work your way into some of the other issues.

I have been doing some work on climate change through the National Roundtable on the Environment and the Economy. The problem with climate change right now is that we have people saying that we are all dead, that the temperature is going up to two to six degrees Centigrade, there will not be any ice caps, there will not be any polar bears, and we are all going to be asphyxiated. Then you have ordinary citizens asking what that has to do with them, as they are driving along the highway in their SUV. Finally, you have the politicians, in between, wondering how to position themselves.

There are a million Aboriginal people in this country, the fastest growing segment of the population, and most of them still live in appalling poverty; and yet, we are going to have huge shortages of skilled labour within the next five years. There is a disconnect there.

Look at what has happened to our cities, for example Toronto over the last seven years under Mike Harris: smog is killing kids; traffic congestion is harming the economy; homelessness is growing. Eighty percent of Canadians live in cities. The global economy is urban. It is service-based. It takes skilled people. Yet, many urban issues are not being addressed. Surely, in a country as wealthy and with the opportunities that we have, we can come to grips with those problems successfully too.

Barb Byers
President
Saskatchewan Federation of Labour

One of the important things about this discussion is the fact that we are having it. Those who have been around for a few years will remember that there was a time that we were not allowed to talk about labour's relationship with the NDP. If we were unhappy with the latter, we did not talk about it. We were not allowed to discuss our relationship in polite company, and in fact not even in impolite company. Some believed that you were not a true trade unionist if you were not an NDP activist; and others believed that you were not a trade unionist if you were an NDP activist. The important part of this discussion is that we are allowing the expression of that diversity of opinion, truly reflecting the diversity of our membership. The latter is not a homogeneous group with a single position.

What is the Canadian experience of the relationship between labour and social-democracy? It is difficult to discuss. There is a federal experience, and then the experiences of the 13 provinces and territories. My own province clearly differs from some others: the NDP has been in power in Saskatchewan for 42 of the last 58 years. I have lived 69 percent of my life under an NDP government.

Over the last couple of days, we have talked a lot about mistresses and, occasionally, about marriages. In Saskatchewan, discussions in our executive and questions to politicians at our conventions show that we are tired of being a mistress. If we are going to be a mistress, we want to be treated well, we would like jewellery, we would like fancy places to live, we would like good lives, and we would like, occasionally, to be taken out for dinner! But the reality for a lot of us has been different.

The tensions between labour and social-democratic governments were linked by some to situations when the party in government acts as an employer in regard to the public sector unions. However, I do not think this is the key issue. In my province, we find from time to time that both the private and the public sectors may be happy or unhappy with the NDP as government. Private-sector unions, in my province at any rate, tend to affiliate more to the NDP, but we also know, from research across Canada, that private-sector union members do not tend to vote NDP. The reverse happens in the public sector. Public-sector unions do not affiliate en masse, but their members tend to vote NDP. That is a contradiction that we really need to deal with.

The other thing we must deal with is the tension between being right and having power. Without power, how can you do some of the things you want to do? How we are going to be able to move things along if we are not in government?

We also need to deal with the claim that there is no alternative. Under the Romanow government in Saskatchewan, we were consistently told: "If you do not like this, do you want me to show you videos of Mike Harris or Ralph Klein?" (Today they could add Campbell in British Columbia.) That is not a way to mobilize people. You cannot go to knock on somebody's door in an election, and say: "Vote NDP, because it is better than the alternative". You have to give something to get people.

Politicians who turn their backs on unions must be made to face the consequences. We do not do a very good job of that. We talk about it a lot, but we do not do what needs to be done. Making politicians face the consequences means, quite frankly, taking them out. Maybe not taking the whole government out, but saying at some point: we are targeting five constituencies, for example, and going after them in a very serious way. Tony Benn says that we should be asking politicians what power they have, how they got it, in whose interests they use it, to whom they are accountable, and, finally, how we can get rid of them.

It is critical for the labour movement to separate the labour program from the party program. Too often, when they get too enmeshed, people ask who the trade-union movement is really defending. That is particularly the case when the NDP is in government. There is confusion and we start to fight with each other. In the trade-union movement in Saskatchewan, fighting about the NDP was like a yearly blood sport at the Federation conventions. We would all line up at the mikes. We did not get much accomplished. It did not mobilize our members. Everybody got their shots in; and it did not unify us. Unfortunately, our memories of each other are very long, and we are consequently much tougher on each other than on either employers or governments.

We have talked about organizing, getting workers involved in our campaigns, stopping telling members whom to vote for, getting back to basics again, and organizing at the work site. Yet, we need to examine whether the organizing that we do on our issues, does in fact help to organize and support the party.

Another of our challenges is to include those who have been excluded. We need to look around and ask who is not included in our movement, notably youth, and Aboriginal people. In my province, this is a critical issue. One in four new labour-force entrants is Aboriginal, as of a couple of years ago. That is our future union membership. Those are also the voters of the future. We have to talk about and include workers of colour and workers with disabilities, and our movement must reflect their participation. Furthermore, let us not lose track of our retirees. Too often, when people quit or retire from their jobs, they are also cut off from being union members and from the information the union provides.

Mike Smith informed us of the impact of proportional representation in his country. We have put forward a resolution at our Federation Convention stat ing that we support proportional representation. Yet, if you went out and asked most of our activists what that really means, I do not know if they would really understand it. I have it down as an item for more detailed discussion next year at our convention.

The last thing is to say that the struggle will continue. We have to keep governments' feet to the fire. That is the critical thing. As Frederick Douglass said: "Power concedes nothing without a demand." As Brother Vavi said: "What you have not won in the streets, you cannot win in Parliament." The members must believe that you are representing them first and we need to put some class back into the struggle. We need to be calling on people and talking about the issues that affect us, as part of the working class. We need to be doing research, with organizations like the Canadian Centre for Policy Alternatives, on who runs our governments and our corporations.

We have a lot of work to do and the real challenge to us is what we do with the ideas we have raised. If we say "Great information!" and do not do anything with it, then we have really defeated our own purpose and have, in fact, demobilized ourselves. It is up to us, individually and politically, inside our organizations, to make sure that something happens with everything that has been said.

Ed Broadbent
Leader (1975 to 1989)
New Democratic Party

I want to restrict my comments to a few significant conclusions that we could draw from these presentations, and that apply to where the party and labour movement should be going here in Canada. I draw three conclusions from our discussion:

1. Labour movements and parties of the left—we have mainly talked about social-democratic parties here, but it applies to other left parties as well—all over have had *mutually-supportive* relationships. That is because we are dealing with the redistribution of power and income. That is what the relationship is all about. The trade-union movement does it within the workplace and the party, in general, does it within society. They are both working for the redistribution of power and income. That is why I do not think that it is an accident, historically, that left parties, trade unions, the democratic franchise, and the industrial system all emerged together. They have retained, as we have seen, certain working relationships that we have heard about here today.

2. They are all different, with rather important nuances—and, in some cases, more than nuances, as we have heard in the last few days. There are different kinds of relationships between the parties and the trade-union movement, but virtually all of the ones that we have heard about are working. We have the great, old, continuing metaphor of the marriage—it is a useful one—but the very fact that you use it, means that there is a serious relationship there.

3. All of the parties and trade-union movements have been responding to a transition from an industrial to a post-industrial economy. That is very important, because that has been the source of tension between the trade-union movement and the party in different parts of the world. As the party has reached out, for example,

to new parts of the labour force, tension has very often arisen between it and the trade-union movement that represents the industrial labour force.

A related point that came through clearly and explicitly, especially from our friends from Europe, is that some countries are doing very well with globalization. They are coping very well, but other developed and many developing countries are not doing so well.

Financial backers of parties of the left are going to be outspent by corporations. As the AFL-CIO pointed out, corporations outspend labour in the States 20 to 1. The ratio is not quite as bad in Canada, but it is serious. The more the world globalizes, the tougher this is going to be. Public opinion is saying that the more collective centres of money, whether unions on the left or corporations on the right, get out of directly financing political agendas in the country, the better things will be. As the Co-Chair of the Corporate Accountability Commission which just completed its work, I can tell you that there is large support in Canada for putting an end to corporate and union contributions to political parties.

We have to supplement the removal of corporate and union funds with spending limits on the parties and other state action to keep politics democratic. As one who has come out of the party structure, as opposed to labour, I believe that both labour and the party have a serious interest in getting money out of directly financing political parties.

The descriptions of party-union relationships elsewhere confirmed a certain tendency I have been moving in myself. When I became a political activist in Oshawa, I believed profoundly in the integrated, structural relationship that emerged between the party and the trade-union movement in most Commonwealth countries. I am now going in the other direction: the more independence between the two, the better. I liked what Guenther Horzetzky said about the situation in Germany. I also liked the AFL-CIO's working-class emphasis and the way that it mobilized the vote south of the border. Frankly, it has done so a lot more successfully than we have done in recent years, with our affiliated structural relationship. They are persuading their members 'on-the-job,' as we used to do in the past. We should therefore look more closely at breaking up the integrated relationship between the party and the trade-union movement—each independent of the other, but working for the same agenda.

The trade-union movement should keep its autonomy, concentrate on the workers within it, both in more narrowly-defined trade union matters—health and safety, salaries, pensions, all of these important things—but also in political education. Whether it's between or during elections, we should do what they are doing in Germany, what they have done in other countries, what they are now doing in the United States, what they used to do in Oshawa, when I was first elected in 1968: the on-the-job canvass. This is how the trade-union movement can make its biggest contribution to a common cause with its members:

- Outline the various parties' programs;
- Make it clear where they stand on real issues that concern workers; and then, of course
- Let workers draw their own conclusions.

Overwhelmingly, they will come to the NDP, if the NDP is doing its job on the issues. An independent structure will allow the union to act politically for its members, while allowing the party to do what it needs to do, which is not only to develop an agenda that includes such important things as workers' rights, taxation policy, and corporate power, but also to reach out to new parts of the labour market, beyond the industrial sector. This kind of reaching out has gone on in continental Europe with great success, so the party here should not be accused of betraying its purpose when it does the same. Quite the contrary, the purpose of the social-democratic party is to speak for workers and that means going beyond traditional categories of workers to new ones, many working in quasi-independence, even in advanced societies, not just in the Brazilian informal sector, but here as well.

Third, the party and the trade-union movement should be coordinating their policies between elections in an informal way, with serious policy people coming together from the trade-union movement and the party, working year in and year out, between elections, on major economic issues. We can do that privately. We do not have to do it publicly. We have to keep our agendas in common so that, when the elections come, we are thinking in broadly similar ways and can campaign, the trade-union movement working within the working sector, and the party reaching out to the broader community. That informal cooperation is important as a continuing effort between the broadly-defined leadership in the trade-union movement and the party.

Finally, it is so important to understand that, in a free society, we are going to differ from time to time. It is inevitable that we are going to have conflict when the party is in government, but that is a glaring example. It is inescapable that there are going to be differences. But there will be differences on other policy matters, too, and what is important is the integrity of relationships between the leadership in the party and the leadership in the various trade unions. The unstated rule—which I am going to state now—is that you do not dump on each other in public. You may—no, you will—have to disagree publicly with each other, from time to time. However you don't need to enter into acrimonious debate or acrimonious criticism. That's the difference.

The practice of mutual respect when we differ occasionally in our common struggle to redistribute power and income in society is crucial to our relationship. We have to make sure that we really do respect the different constituencies that we each come from, try to have the debates in private first and, if there is going to be a difference in public, damn well make sure that it is civil.

Wayne Samuelson
President
Ontario Federation of Labour

I have spent most of my life as a political organizer, within the party and within the community. While I find this discussion stimulating, it is equally frustrating, because the measure for me is what kind of impact this discussion has on working people and on people in the community that I come from, in east-end Kitchener, who cannot find jobs and see the government turning its back on them. In my 20 years in a tire factory, not once did I sit down in the morning to have a coffee and hear the guy beside me take a sip of his coffee and ask me what I thought about neo-liberalism. To those people, right and left is the answer that you get when you roll down the window and ask somebody how to get somewhere. Sometimes, we need to think a little bit about what this means. There is not a lot of debate about affiliation or one-member-one-vote among a lot of those people. What it is really about for them is: what does all of this mean to me, my family and my community?

Things would be a lot different if the NDP were not there and the labour movement had not made a decision a long time ago to help build it. Traditionally, it is the NDP—whether in government, in opposition, or even pressuring a minority government—which has raised the issues that are important to us, such as rent control, housing, income support, or other union issues. Those issues would not be on the public agenda without the NDP. We need to remember that and think about what the world would be like without it. Under our parliamentary system, it is important to have seats in the House.

There is an incredibly interesting debate in the labour movement about whether to be involved in coalition politics or in party politics. My experience in campaigns in Manitoba, British Columbia, and other parts of Canada, tells me that the same people are usually involved in both. The party organizers also usually participate in the coalition. At the Federation, we are working right now with over sixty organizations, trying to develop some kind of a vision for the province.

If there is one thing that we need to do, it is to take some chances—to take a chance on building the NDP, to take a chance that we may have a debate that will anger some people. At the end of the day, if we do not do it, there are not a lot of people out there who have the resources and capability to do so.

We started to talk about how to build a party. But I wake up in the morning thinking about how to make a difference. You know, a guy froze on the street a block and a half from where I live. We have a government that is not building housing, that has destroyed rent controls, and that is what we have to think about, people like him, who need us. People like the woman I talked to in Thunder Bay, who told me that her son in grade five cannot get access to special education, and will suffer for the rest of his life because of that. There is nothing wrong with debate, but maybe it is time that we engaged in some real action.

You do not do that by debating internal party structures. You do not do it by debating about who is more right or who is more left. You do it by getting down to the work of rolling up your sleeves and getting our activists involved in the NDP, but also in a whole range of other groups. If I can leave you with one thought, it is that a lot of people came before us and they built something that has made a difference to millions of people in their everyday life. We can debate for the next twenty years whether we want to continue what they began or what is wrong with it, but if we do not get moving on rebuilding our party, this discussion will not be taking place thirty years from now, because all that has been built will be destroyed.

Howard Pawley
Premier of Manitoba (1981 to 1988)

We bear a tremendous onus, as activists within the labour movement and New Democratic Party, to ensure that we get it right this time and that we develop processes and the means by which we can proceed to act:

1. on behalf of those who are disadvantaged;
2. on behalf of the labour membership;
3. on behalf of the vast majority of people.

It is about time that we assumed this challenge and ensured that we develop these necessary processes.

First and foremost, it is critically important that we recognize, insofar as the labour-New Democratic relationship is concerned, that there should be no winners or losers at the expense of the other. We must all share in the winning; it is possible. We are proud of the fact that the New Democratic Party has governed for 18 of the past 33 years in Manitoba. The NDP and the labour movement in the province must be doing something right. In 1983, Gary Doer was the head of the Manitoba Government Employees' Union (MGEU) when it agreed upon a social contract with the provincial government. I am sure that hardly any of you realize that there was a social contract in the Province of Manitoba. We worked it out over a period of two to three days with the participation of the leadership of all the parties: I was involved with some of my Cabinet Ministers and the leadership of the MGEU. The union obtained ratification for the social contract deal from its membership and I recall walking down the steps of the legislature to the pressroom when Gary Doer proudly declared that he had achieved 87 percent membership ratification in support of the proposed deal. I replied, "Gary, please do not mention that at the press conference. It won't make the government look particularly good." He listened. He has never mentioned the 87 percent support. But it came about as a result of an overriding relationship of trust and understanding between labour and the New Democratic Party in the Province of Manitoba.

Secondly, we must be prepared to accept and expect diversity of views within our ranks. I emphasize this, because what I have found most difficult, in the New Democratic Party and, before it, in CCF circles, is the reality of the ideological intolerance we often express to each other. Somebody is either too right-wing, too left-wing, or too utopian. We should rather accept the fact that we are a diverse party and we should encourage diverse points of view. In 1972, when the Ontario party expelled the Waffle, Ed Schreyer told the Manitoba party's convention: "We will have none of that. We want a hundred flowers to bloom in the Province of Manitoba. We must not get all uptight when we are part of a NDP government, because some people from the labour movement demonstrate against us or criticize us." I have to tell you very candidly that I was pleased when I sometimes received criticism from the left. There is an excess of criticism from the right and it is sometimes beneficial to have some criticism from the left to balance things out. I do not know why we get so uptight, individually and collectively, over that kind of thing. I have never understood it and never will. Diversity is extremely important.

Thirdly, the processes we develop to communicate with each other are extremely important. Neither labour, nor the NDP leadership may ambush each other. I was fortunate. I had an advantage that most other NDP leaders did not enjoy. I worked with Dick Martin and you could not find anyone more trustworthy than Dick Martin. We often disagreed, but, when we did disagree, we had first thoroughly discussed our disagreement. Neither ambushed the other and labour participated in every stage of government. It was not shut out. We had monthly labour liaison meetings where particular irritants concerning the labour movement were dealt with. We had an Election Planning Committee on which a labour representative served. Cabinet ministers and caucus members frequently met labour members for input.

Some have explained the relationship by pointing to an interesting opportunity that existed for social interaction. The Union Centre was a few blocks from the Legislature, so it was not uncommon for one cabinet minister or another to be at the Centre every Friday, having a beer and chatting with leaders of the union movement about the latest issues confronting the government. Yes! With all of the structures and processes we put in place, it made a difference. Process is very important and let us not forget it.

Fourthly, as Zwelinzima Vavi put it: "Let us not put all of our eggs in one basket." That means that we must build the alliances necessary to carry on the total campaign we must undertake to transform society. Coalitions are important. We must build research facilities that will support us. The Health Coalitions and the Canadian Centre for Policy Alternatives are excellent examples.

Fifth, how should we co-operate in election campaigns? Labour and the party should run parallel campaigns. In 1981 and 1986, one of the major reasons for our successful election was the tremendous number of phone banks organized by the trade-union movement. They canvassed their members in their homes and spoke personally to them, one on one. I am not sure that we would have won in 1981 and 1986 but for that contribution by labour.

It is important that we speak to members' concerns, that we recognize the importance of the short term and the long term, that we recognize that we probably all have similar long-term objectives. However, we recognize that there are short-term goals, too. There is a statement of principles at the back of the NDP membership card. It describes our long-term objectives and everyone in this room would be pleased with them, both left and right. Nonetheless, we also recognize that there are short-term practicalities we face. We have too frequently lost sight of the long-term objectives, while dealing only with the short-term emergencies. We have to assure our membership that we have a vision—the New Jerusalem, as Tommy Douglas used to describe it.

Ed Broadbent has raised the question of affiliation. I participated in the NDP's founding convention and vividly recall the debate that raged between those supporting formula A and formula B (the two alternatives proposed for the future role of affiliated organizations within the NDP). I remain unsure whether the correct formula was eventually chosen. Maybe we should go back and look at the experience of the past 42 years and relate it to the present time. I was part of the anti-establishment opposition within the party at the time. The Manitoba party, by the way, was nearly equally divided. Ed Schreyer was elected President by three votes and was seen to be tending in favour of the establishment of the party. I was elected the Vice-President of the party at the same Convention by only two votes and was seen to be on the opposite side of Ed Schreyer on the affiliation issue.

I am very worried about how turned off young people are by political parties. I am very aware of this at the university level where I teach. Young people who five, ten, twenty years ago, would have been members of the New Democrats, have little or no confidence in the political system, even though they are more to the left than they were, and there are more of them. It will not be easy, but we must discover ways to attract those young people on the left back into the party. We must also discuss the role of the party's provincial sections within the federal party.

Lastly, we should be having this kind of discussion within the New Democratic Party, and then bringing the New Democratic Party and the Canadian Labour Congress together, in order to ensure that we maintain this process and that we get it right this time. We got it wrong in 1961.

Buzz Hargrove
President
Canadian Auto Workers

We are in a crisis as a party and the labour movement in Canada is part of that problem. The polls show that we are not relevant to the Canadian people either federally or provincially. We are not relevant to the labour movement as a party, as we used to be at one time. We are not relevant to union members and we are not bringing new activists in. I should not say *any* because, of course, there is always the odd one, but, compared to when we were on the move, there has been a major, major change.

We have a problem. Let me first deal with the party. The challenge is for us to rise to the occasion and be as radical, or more radical, than the right, who have been incredibly radical, over the last couple of decades in Canada, over every issue that they wanted, from deregulation, to privatization, to undermining the role of government, to denigrating the role of people who work in the public sector.

Nothing infuriates me more than to see Premier Ralph Klein say to teachers that they only work a couple of hours a day. Mike Harris said the same thing. I was at a conference of my own union in Port Elgin on Saturday morning. It was a weekend introduction to a course that we had and people were invited to bring their spouses in for the opening session. One of the spouses with whom I spoke said that she did not want to tell me where she worked, that she was not a member of my union. I said: "Well, that is no reason not to tell me where you work," and she replied: "I work in the public sector. People hate government and public-sector workers so much that I do not feel comfortable telling people where I work." You know, that's a damn sin in a country like ours that has relied so much on the public sector to make it what it is today. My guess is that she is not the only one, if you watch what is happening to public-sector workers across the country.

So we have to challenge, we have to be more radical, and we have to be absolutely clear on who we are, whom we represent, whom we want to represent, and what we want to accomplish. We cannot just be an electoral machine and hope that we can come to power. Over the last two decades, we have watched the most massive transfer of wealth in our history, from the poorest in our society to the wealthiest.

Have we got the issues today! We have opportunities like we have never had. But we have to stand up first and say: We are the party of government—not big government, not wasteful government, but government on behalf of the people, a counterbalance to the powerful corporations who drive the Liberals, and the Tories, and the Alliance, and the other right-wingers in this country. One can only imagine what would have happened if one of Bob Rae's first acts, when he was elected Premier, had been to introduce government auto insurance, which we campaigned on, but backed away from—Bob Rae backed away, not our party. Bob Rae backed away and said: Government is not the party. I do not give a damn what the party says. Government is going to do whatever the hell it wants, once in power. Imagine if he had moved ahead on that. Why did people elect us if it was so radical? He should not have introduced his social contract, which was very different than the one that Howard Pawley talked about. When you abuse the power of government against working people, then you do not deserve the support of working people.

In Manitoba recently, one of the wealthiest capitalists in the province put our people on the street. They had walked the picket line for twenty-five years to win the contract they had, and he said that he did not want to bargain with them, that he was not going to settle the contract, but to move his operation to North Dakota, a right-wing state. I said to Gary Doer and his government that they should nationalize the son of a bitch. He should not have the right to remove from the province a farm-equipment industry or, in this case, a product, that was developed by government research and development money—$32 million in loans from the federal government of Canada and millions pumped into the operation by the Manitoba government. But we could not even talk about it. The idea of government ownership was dismissed out of hand. If you cannot step in to defend workers when they are in crisis, why would workers turn to those people when it comes election time? I can tell you that Gary Doer had a lot of good friends in that workplace. They would not vote NDP again for the life of them.

Now, we can ignore all of those things and think that everything is going fine, but I believe that there is a time when you have to stand up and be counted. There are defining moments in the life of a political party, as there are in a labour movement or any movement. That was such a moment in Manitoba, just as auto insurance was in Ontario, much like health care or Medicare was with Tommy Douglas, in Saskatchewan and later federally. Was it controversial when Tommy Douglas brought in medicare!

Both the party and the labour movement need to understand our history. I get so sick of hearing that labour does not get the vote out, as though that was the commitment of the labour movement in the early days. That was not what the marriage of the party and labour was about. It was about two progressive organizations coming together, with all kinds of very diverse ideas. Labour had this institution that could provide opportunity to the party leadership beyond anything that they had imagined: opening up the doors of union halls to invite them into meetings; signing people up in the party once they had convinced them that this was their party; and using our structures to give them an opportunity to educate our members and their families.

Our structure allowed us to do things. We had people in place to carry out campaigns. We could go out and knock on doors. We could get people out to vote. That was labour's commitment, along with money and resources to allow the party to do the things that a political party has to do. All that has changed today and it is allegedly labour's fault, because we cannot deliver the vote. I am sorry. The party is the one missing the boat. The party has to get people excited about what it stands for, what its issues are, and which programs it wants people to vote for.

We can get the voters out. We do so now. We do a hell of a lot better at mobilizing and getting people out to vote. Our problem is that they have been voting Liberal, Tory, and Reform/Alliance in recent years. There are more working-class families and more union members voting in Canada than in the United States, and, if we only had two capitalist parties, which some people are promoting in Canada, or three or four capitalist parties, maybe we would do better to get them out, I do not know.

But one thing that they will not do is to vote for the NDP as it is today. We have to decide whether we are a capitalist party and want to go out and try to compete with the capitalists, or whether we want to be a Democratic-Socialist party, a party of the left that appeals to people, based on what is important to us as a movement.

The other issue over which I disagree with Ed Broadbent is this idea of criticism. Howard Pawley hit the nail on the head. I remember when the Trudeau government brought in wage controls and received the support of Schreyer and Blakeney. Did the labour movement ever hammer them across the country on those issues! That did not destroy or harm our party. Debate and differences of opinion on issues, I would argue, are what built our parties. Solidarity in silence or solidarity in decline, as I refer to it, brought us to where we are at today and will be what defeats us. If we cannot get our issues out and deal with them then we will never get over this period and grow as a party.

People say that the labour movement brings down the party. There was a recent, right-wing study on the support for labour unions in Canada. They said that it is at its highest in over 40 years, going back to the 1960s. Over 60 percent of Canadians support labour unions; over 91 percent of members of private-sector unions support their union; 83 percent of public-sector workers support their union. We ought to ask the party to support labour and become the party ourselves! We are way, way ahead in the polls. We have much more support amongst the public and the working people of the country and we cannot ignore that.

We have to end the institutional relationship between the labour movement and the party. I do not subscribe to the belief that we made a mistake in 1961, but political parties evolve, the labour movement has evolved, the workplace has evolved, the economy has changed quite radically, and people's thinking is different. Of course we could keep on going as we have been, on the grounds that the party is better than the right-wing alternatives. I get this thrown at me all the time: would you not sooner have Bob Rae than Mike Harris? When I was in the UK a few months ago, people were saying they were better off to have Blair than Maggie Thatcher. My guess is that people in New Zealand would say that they are a lot better off with Helen Clark. Most working people in British Columbia today would probably say they would sooner have Glen Clark back than Gordon Campbell. But that does not build for the future. People say that, if we wait long enough, the pendulum will swing. That is not good enough. We have to build for the future. But we cannot do that with the kinds of divisions that we have today, and not just between the party and the labour movement (which causes enormous tension constantly), but within the labour movement itself.

We have this pro-NDP group in the labour movement that does not give a damn what the NDP does. That is not where I think we should be as a movement. Our relationship with political parties has to mean more than that. I am not offended that people should feel that way in our movement. I respect knowing where they are at, but how do we build on such a position? As Howard Pawley said, how do we bring together this diverse organization of the left and progressives across the country and move ahead? I do not think that we can do it if we have this institutional link that has us constantly feuding with one another. I believe that we need a party that is financed by government and limited individual donations, much along the lines that Quebec and Manitoba have in place. I did not join the party as a member of my local union. I joined the party as Buzz Hargrove. What brought me in was the opportunity presented to me to listen to people like Tommy Douglas and David Lewis, and later Ed Broadbent, and others in our movement. We will have a lot more credibility as a movement—and, as was suggested, parallel campaigns—when we campaign on *issues*, and the party decides if those are the issues that it wants to promote, then develops a campaign parallel to labour's on those issues.

We have to open up our party and reach out. I was not impressed by what happened at the Convention in Winnipeg, for several reasons. But the main one was that I thought that we would have had an opportunity to embrace a much larger group of progressive people on the left in this country if more time had been spent talking prior to the Convention, bringing those people together, and recognizing that changes have to be made.

But it is still not too late. We have to identify whom we want to represent, make a clear choice between those with wealth and power, or those without wealth, the underprivileged, those without power or even a voice in our institutions across the country. We need to institute individual memberships, limited individual and government financing. Labour has the credibility, believe me. The right would have undermined the labour movement in Canada if they had been able to. They could not, because the support is there for unions.

Do you know where we fall apart? I do not know how many times I get told: Buzz, I support what you guys do as a union. I support the labour movement. I even support the NDP, but I will be damned if I am going to support you guys if you keep giving money to the NDP from the guy who works next to me, who does not support them. That is the single most, divisive issue facing us today.

We can move ahead with a party built on individual memberships that is challenging and credible to the labour movement. We could encourage more labour activists and leaders to join the party, if it were a clear, left party, with ideals and principles that we can be proud of, a party that has credibility and integrity once in government. You cannot campaign on something and then not do it.

The right surely—I feel sick when I say it—showed us that. Mike Harris said what he was going to do. I do not like it, but he campaigned on it, he got elected and he carried through with it—at least he did what he said that he would do. It is time that our party had that kind of credibility.

Concluding Remarks

Alexa McDonough
Leader
New Democratic Party of Canada

At the end of the day, what becomes very clear is that politics is practised within a particular context and within a particular culture. There are dynamics that exist at a point in time in any country or any geographic area. The challenges are really quite specific. At the same time, there were many common threads in the presentations. For us, the real work begins from this point forward. What can we learn from all this? The NDP is about at the mid-point in a major process of reflection and renewal and the CLC is involved in a similar process on a kind of parallel track. There is a tremendous need for a responsible, reflective, and respectful dialogue between the party and the labour movement concerning their future relationship and how best to accomplish our shared objectives.

I have always been a fervent, passionate believer in an important, strong, working relationship between the New Democratic Party and the labour movement and, more specifically, a believer in the partnership that launched the New Democratic Party. When I sought the federal leadership of the NDP, I said that if I had my way, there would not be a divorce. I believed that strongly in 1995. I believe no less passionately today in the importance of a strong, working relationship between the labour movement and a social-democratic party. Of course, there is no one formula for what that relationship should look like. But I have never heard, in my twenty-two years in politics, about a social democratic party that fared well or achieved any measure of success without having had a solid working relationship with the labour movement. I am also unaware of any examples of a labour movement having improved the lives of working people in the absence of a solid, left-wing political presence in the electoral field, preferably in government, but, if not, in as strong a position as possible in opposition.

Nothing has changed my mind about this. At the same time, we all recognize that we are not getting the results that we want from our current relationship. It is thus absolutely critical that we put the latter under a microscope and discuss it further.

Secondly, I agree with Buzz Hargrove's statement that we need this discussion to be forward-looking. We need to be building for the future. We have to learn from the past, but, for the love of God, let us not keep hashing and rehashing the1990-1995 years in Ontario. Let us not keep fighting and rehashing every past election. Let us learn what we need to learn, and let us get on with the discussions and the debates, and figure out where we need to go from here.

Thirdly, we have to look closely at how we use the media and how the media uses us. Much of what we do is not reported. For example, some have expressed frustration because they did not feel that the New Democratic Party caucus was doing very much on environmental issues. Some have pointed to the efforts by the Federation of Canadian Municipalities (FCM) to win support in seeking more federal dollars, a commitment to a Major Cities project, and support for public transit in order to contribute to the reduction of greenhouse gases. I feel defensive saying this but, for the record—and I say it to try to make a point about our relationship with the media—in November we invited the FCM to meet with the federal caucus. They were delighted to accept. We are still the only federal party, the only caucus, to have met with the FCM. Do you know why? Because, after our meeting, they felt that as a non-partisan organization they ought to meet with the other party caucuses as well. Three months later, they are still waiting for a reply from the other four parties. We have been working with the FCM on these issues and will go on doing so. There is hardly any group with which I have spent more time talking in the broad political arena, than representatives of municipalities, in an attempt to make sustainability issues real, concrete and practical, and to make sure that we are working together around them.

My point is that you are not going to read about this in the papers, but it is not because we do not put it out there. If people want to see us doing more in a given area, they should not assume that we are not already doing it, because they have not read about it in the papers.

Evidently, we need to do a better job on our communications. This was stated forcefully at the meetings across the country during the first phase of our renewal process. The message was heard loudly and clearly. I can assure you that we are striving to improve with the active participation of the CLC and its affiliated unions.

We also know that, if the New Democratic Party or a labour leader want to get a headline in the newspaper on any day of the week, all they have to do is attack each other. It is the cheapest, easiest way to get coverage. Nancy Riche works her guts out on behalf of the labour movement, as the Associate President of the New Democratic Party. I do not want to tell any tales out of school here. We have many discussions, sometimes differing and disagreeing on decisions that get reached, but we do not go out and beat up on each other through the media. We depend upon diverse views being contributed to the debate and then getting on with implementing the decisions that get made and being accountable for them. We cannot advance the important, respectful debate we need, through what is clearly a hostile medium, the corporate controlled media.

Finally, with respect to the very difficult issue of reforming political-party financing, while it is problematic when the New Democratic Party is in government, it is even more so in the context of the NDP-labour relationship federally. In abstract terms, everyone agrees that we would all benefit if there were a way to level the playing field. The statistics provided by the AFL-CIO demonstrate that unions cannot match funds donated by the corporate sector. The difficulty for us lies in the implementation of reforms in party financing. Were the labour movement and the NDP to agree that the latter would accept no more union or corporation contributions, we would unilaterally disarm ourselves and put both hands behind our back. We would cut off a tremendously important source of funding to the New Democratic Party, while the corporations just continued to fund the other parties massively.

I would like to conclude by saying how enormously indebted I feel personally, and as Leader of the Federal New Democratic Party for the last six years, to the Canadian Labour Congress. I speak for all of my colleagues in this. The CLC has always been there for us through thick and thin. Were it not for the CLC and its major affiliates, the Federal New Democratic Party would never have re-established official party status in 1997. There was a flood of support to the party leading up to the 1997 election. We were very proud of the fact that, among the 16 new members we elected in 1997, eight men and eight women, ten were trade unionists. Although we have heard many stories about elected trade unionists, from various countries, who have, in some way, violated their fundamental trade union principles or their commitments to the trade-union movement, I can say without fear of contradiction that those ten trade unionists who were elected in 1997 with magnificent support from the CLC, never, ever forgot who helped to put them there or, in any way, abandoned their commitments to the trade-union movement.

In the eighty-five public meetings we held across Canada, as part of our renewal process over the last year, only a very few people suggested that the relationship with the trade-union movement was not every bit as important as it ever was. I firmly believe in its importance. Yet, this is not to advocate the status quo. The status quo is not on. We need to find new ways to make the relationship more effective. I look forward to the continuing respectful dialogue between the party and the labour movement.

Ken Georgetti
President
Canadian Labour Congress

Labour unions have always sought very clearly to represent the interests of workers to their employers and, unless workers can feel it in their stomachs—unless they can feel that we have made progress to make them better off, to make their lives better—then we cannot go anywhere else with our action.

The first time I had the opportunity to vote, I was not a New Democrat. My Dad was, but I said that was his party. I wanted cheaper auto insurance. That is what motivated me to vote for the Dave Barrett government at the time, and they gave me cheaper auto insurance. I voted with my wallet. I wanted a deal and they attracted my attention.

Over time, each of us, from our different, historical backgrounds, discovered that we also had a motivation to be politically active. In every country and every generation, we seem to have to rediscover how to get people active and interested. In BC, the labour movement worked hard to elect Mike Harcourt's NDP government. Over the years, Mike Harcourt became a personal hero of mine as I learned how important it was to work with a government that shares your political beliefs. One year after Brother Harcourt was elected, we had automatic certification by cards and anti-scab legislation in British Columbia, something that he had promised to do and he delivered at the first chance that he got. I know that Jim Sinclair, the current BC Federation of Labour President, will not be able to say the same on the one-year anniversary of the Campbell government, I am sure. Probably it will be gone by then. British Columbia workers are starting now to understand that political action and political activism are in their own self-interest.

In Canada, we have done everything from presenting briefs to governments to forming political parties, as a way to meet the challenges that have faced us. Those challenges remain as large today as they were when trade unionists set out to lobby governments for their legal right to organize and bargain collectively for workers in the 19th century.

The world has changed since 1961, when the Canadian Labour Congress participated actively in the creation of the NDP. Both we and the party are searching for how best to be politically effective, politically relevant and, indeed, politically successful. It has changed even for those who live in provinces with NDP governments. The relationship that Rod Hilliard and the Manitoba Federation of Labour have with Premier Gary Doer is not the same as the relationship that his forerunner Dick Martin had with Premier Howard Pawley.

This discussion has allowed us to see that we are not alone in these challenges. It has allowed us to think outside the box and, indeed, it has allowed our contributors to think outside their usual framework of action. I believe that this discussion is an example of how we have to think globally, but act locally, both as a labour movement and as a political movement.

In Canada, we know that the status quo is not working. Both labour and the party have been, and continue to be, engaged in reviews and renewal debates. We know that Labour needs a party in this country that represents workers' views and promotes the dreams and aspirations that challenge us, as trade union activists, every day.

Buzz Hargrove spoke of the poll in which we scored high on every measure of our effectiveness as a labour movement. There was one exception, and that was on the question as to whether labour should endorse a political party. If we are not credible on what we deliver, we cannot give people advice on what to do.

We are committed to participation in the ongoing NDP renewal. We will continue our own review with an open mind. We are determined, as a movement, to find a solution for Canadian families. It is a solution that will lead our members to claim and to realize their self-interest, political awareness, and political action, because, in the end, when political awareness makes our members politically active, this country can only get better and this world can only be a better place.